Envisioning
the garden

Robert Mallet

Envisioning
the garden

Line, Scale, Distance, Form, Color, and Meaning

Translated by Bryan Woy

Drawings by Yves Poinsot

W. W Norton & Company
New York • London

Preceding page: Rose 'Gardener's Pink', catnip, and lady's mantle—a fine color composition by Elizabeth Bullivant. (Stourton House Flower Garden, England)

Opposite: Sea holly (*Eryngium* x *oliverianum*) and daisy bush (*Senecio greyi*) at Tintinhull House (England) during Penelope Hobhouse's time there.

To Corinne, Alice, Thierry, and Daphne, wonderful companions along the way

Contents

Introduction

"When will I be the owner of a little house surrounded by cherry trees? Close by there would be a garden, an orchard, a meadow, a stream bordered by hazels, and my desires would never pass beyond that stream." Jean-Pierre Claris de Florian (*Galatée*, 1783)

More and more of our contemporaries are interested in the world of gardens. Not only are they more likely to visit gardens, but many are also engaged in creating gardens of their own.

Ever wider dissemination of knowledge related to the theme of the garden leads people these days to ask genuine questions of a cultural nature. "What style can I give to my garden?"

Recent discoveries about brain function and the transmission of information by optical means have provided a new point of view, allowing us to make reasoned choices to personally adapt our environment.

When the Prince de Ligne wrote *Coup d'Oeil sur Beloeil* in 1781, he only partly realized the vanity of quarrels about style: gardens *à la française* versus English-style gardens. Because the issue is much more serious than it might seem, it affects people's well-being in all the places where they lead their lives—work, school, university, home—and it determines the design of interior as well as exterior decor. Even zookeepers have understood the need to pay careful attention to their residents' environment if they want to keep them healthy.

Why have those in charge of our public spaces or our work environments failed to grasp the importance of this factor for the quality of their fellow citizens' lives?

We should, instead, try to understand how human vision "works"; which optical effects open up broad prospects to the human spirit, and which ones, in contrast, lock it up in a cage, however gilded it may be. Contrary to the idea that you can do anything and everything in terms of art, the human "machine" is, for example, equipped with a pair of eyes placed on the front of the head and not the back! We respond to certain shapes and certain colors on the basis of some innate mechanisms, but also on the basis of some that are acquired. We need to know and use these in order to achieve the degree of development to which each of us is entitled. In this book we have tried to gather together many observations, organizing them according to the best available knowledge. Some facts have been proven scientifically, others are still unexplained. The main concern is to show, using pictures rather than words, some phenomena that should inspire future gardeners in their creative work.

Vision is a complex phenomenon in which the subjective part impinges heavily on the objective, to the point that the boundary between literal and figurative meanings of the word *vision* itself tends to become blurred. The garden has a number of dimensions: three that we use to locate ourselves in space; then the hours of the day and night, each with its own particular light; then the dimension of time measured by the growth of plants; but above all the sensitivity of the observer. This dimension is so personal that it is largely exclusive to each individual.

Everyone should be able to glean from these pages some original ideas not only to match their tastes, but also to begin to understand how and why it works that way.

One curved line amid the vertical lines
of a copse can evoke real emotion.
(Bois des Moutiers)

*"Now breaks, or now directs,
th' intending Lines."*

Alexander Pope (*Epistle to several Persons*, Epistle IV, 1731)

Lines and punctuation

There is nothing more annoying than a vertical telegraph pole that spoils a whole view, or a fence that crosses a beautiful landscape. Just one straight line crossing our field of vision can overwhelm the whole space. How much more painful, then, are the bars of a prisoner's cage—a prison that can enclose the mind as well as the body? In this way the rigid architecture of some cities can turn city-dwellers into total strangers to the countryside.

Basics

The retina of our eye is made up of two types of sensory cells: one (cones) to tell us "everything is fine, there is no obstacle in view," and the other, more primitive (rods), to say "look out, or you'll trip on the edge of the curb."

We first learned to write using lines and circles, the basis of most forms of writing (left). We also learned to count, and we may observe that Arabic numerals consist of lines forming angles in increasing numbers: number 1, one angle; number 2, two angles; and so on.

At a very early age babies learn to recognize and mentally store enough more or less angled "lines" or features of the face (eyebrows, hair) and remarkable "points" (eyes, mouth) to be able to recognize those around them; and a little later on, not just people's faces but their portraits, too.

Early on, each individual acquires a set of visual markers that will stay in the memory forever: the lines of a landscape, a type of vegetation. If life separates us from our place of origin, we will always have nostalgic memories of it and will try to reproduce a similar effect in our new surroundings. This basic functioning, based on simple lines and points, influences the whole of our lives and how we position ourselves in space.

It is impossible to insist enough on how important lines are in a garden, as are all visual markers. Because without them, the eye goes looking in a series of "jerks" for a "sign" that the memory can recognize. Another person can easily observe this rapid movement of the eyes. Research into the functioning of vision has shown that the short-term memory immediately erases all that the eye has seen briefly but has failed to recognize.

A garden without any line, design, picturesque plant, or significant object leaves no trace in the memory, except perhaps for a strong feeling of frustration, together with a bad headache. Thus we find complete justification for the visual ordering of space into lines and points.

The "Ha-Ha" or "Saut-de-Loup" allows a continuous view of the landscape.

Other useful observations about lines

We need to distinguish here between straight and curved lines, and between horizontal and vertical or diagonal lines. It is sometimes said that a curved line draws the eye farther out, while a straight line shuts it in. A subjective idea for some; more of a subversive one for others! A curve gently invites us to follow its path, while the stiffness and hardness of a straight line repel the eye: it is in some way threatening, synonymous with danger or prohibition. To get rid of fences and other straight barriers, landscapers have used the "Ha-Ha" or "Saut-de-loup", a ditch with steep banks to stop livestock from getting in or out (illustration above).

The horizontal line of a hedge can be softened by pruning it into waves (photo opposite: hedge created by Piet Oudolf). Gaudi used the curved lines he observed in nature to break up the sharp appearance of angles in his architecture. Many landscape architects have taken up the same idea by pruning box and holly in this way. In doing so, they are simply repeating a practice commonly used in Japanese Zen gardens.

Vertical and diagonal lines are essential for any garden. When such lines are curved, they touch the emotions all the more. (Photo at left: *Magnolia kobus* with sinuous branches at Bois des Moutiers).

Therefore whenever we go to a nursery to choose young trees to plant, we must select the form of their branches very carefully and even regularly prune them into the desired shape throughout their growth. In the same way as selecting subjects for bonsai, it is only by choosing from a large number of seedlings that we find the exceptional specimen that one day everyone will admire.

We are also extremely sensitive to all lines forming angles with the horizontal, however small they may be. This is how we can see whether a picture is straight when we hang it on a wall. This is also why it is so important to position a plant before planting it permanently, because any unpleasantly slanting line will be immediately obvious if it does not look right. We must pay particular attention to the choice of lines in the garden.

Symmetrical or balanced

Symmetry, the geometrical arrangement that is said to correspond to the French way of thinking, has a less well-known alternative: the apparent balance of masses. When two groups of objects have a similar visual weight, this generally satisfies the observer without any need for the strict and simplistic application of pure symmetry.

An alternative to pure symmetry, the concept of balance provides a similar level of satisfaction for the mind.

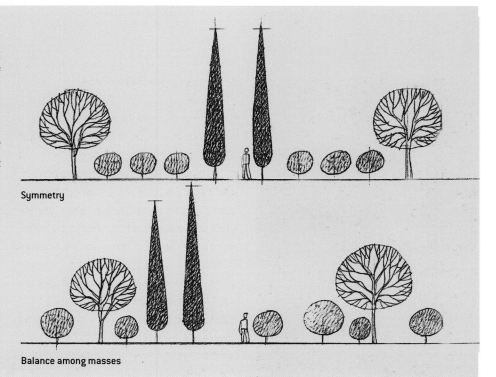

Symmetry

Balance among masses

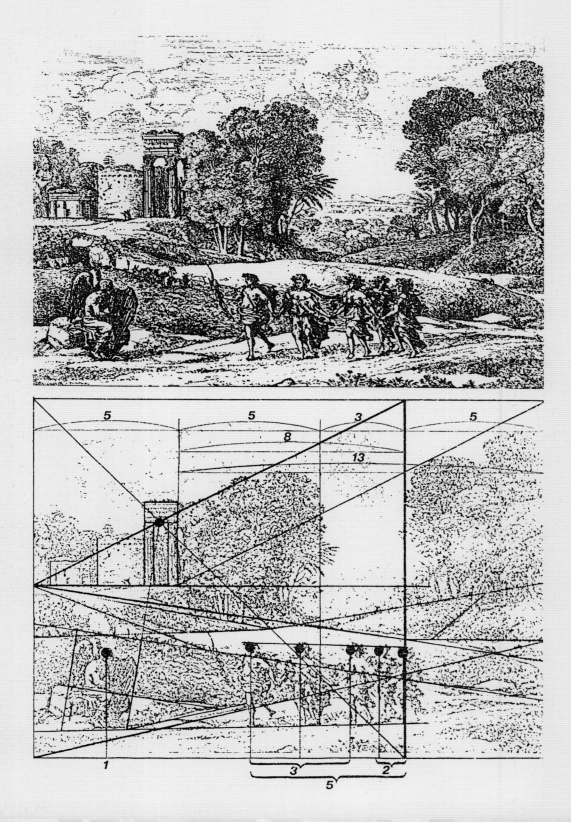

A garden should be composed like a painting: the choice of diagonals is of prime importance. As in this picture by Claude Gellée (known as Claude Lorrain), the main points of interest are found where the oblique lines intersect.

Beyond time and space, the immutability of pure
proportions is a source of deep satisfaction. Just
like a painting, this view opens out onto distant hills,
whose lines are echoed in those of the garden, and
the nearby village church tower, which lies at the
intersection of the composition's lines of force.
(The Garden House, Buckland Monachorum)

A sinuous line curves through the flower beds,
emphasizing the contours and encouraging
the eye to scan tirelessly over this rich winter
composition. (Howard Rice)

A central line focusing the attention only makes sense if it marks a passageway. Otherwise it should be moved or hidden. (below left: Jardin de Saboutot)

Beware the line that drives you crazy!

Just one misplaced line can make life unbearable. A telegraph pole can be hidden by a climbing plant. It can also be disguised by placing a tree with a similar vertical trunk in front of, or even behind, it (photo, below right).

With a badly positioned row of columns, there is a risk of finding one of them right in the middle of the main focal point, focusing the attention to no purpose (illustration at left).

In contrast, a column used as a central focus in the middle of an allée receding into the distance is very original. It urges the eye to look beyond and go farther (photo, below left). Certain sticklers for visual order cannot stand off-center, asymmetric lines that are contrary to logic. For them, it is an unforgivable sin to cut the point off a wedge of Brie or to divide an apple pie off-center into asymmetrical slices: a sign of visual impairment or even sheer rudeness.

All the same, the "almost" and "not quite," like a vertical line "almost in the middle" of a picture, has the power to draw the attention in a way that can sometimes be useful.

Structured design or soft focus

For many, design is the only consideration. For others, structure does not matter so long as there is exhilaration and rapture. One cannot help thinking of a wonderful painting by Turner in the Louvre; it attracted everyone's eyes, standing out from all the many other works with which it was displayed. These were all nevertheless well structured and well drawn, but less attractive.

Shapes and colors do not travel via the same brain pathways; this explains the stylistic differences between artists, such as Turner or Durer, or between landscape gardeners, such as Gertrude Jekyll and Le Nôtre.

Proponents of one of these options, whether "all structure" or "all color," are rarely able to appreciate the other; yet it is often a measured balance between the rigor of a structured design and a great abundance of vegetation that stimulates real pleasure. It could be said, then, that the design of a garden is like a musical staff, while the plants provide the notes of the melody.

"The majestic boredom of symmetry has suddenly made us jump from one extreme to another. If symmetry had for too long a time imposed a badly understood order to shut everything in, irregularity soon took disorder too far in the other direction, losing the view in vagueness and confusion."

(René-Louis de Girardin, *De la Composition des Paysages*, 1775)

Left, top: An "all structure" garden. (*Le Grand Courtoiseau*)

Left, bottom: An "all color" garden. (*The Garden House*)

Blurring angles and sharp edges

It is fortunate that the brain does not record all the lines and angles we see in our surroundings, for otherwise we would soon reach a state of total saturation. Similarly, it is essential for us to mentally erase most of the noise we hear in our everyday lives. The geometric angular lines of the built environment that we inhabit can sometimes impose themselves in an onerous way and need to be masked or softened.

Above: In this garden everything combines to soften the strong lines of the construction: the plants and the arrangement of the stones. (Mark W. Brown)

Right: Similarly, the spurges (*Euphorbia characias*) at the foot of this fence mitigate its rigor and retain our attention at the same time. (Jardin Plume)

Elucidating the structures

A flower bed devoid of forms cannot be seen properly. This is the effect we find in gardens containing a lot of ground-cover plants when they have been left to their own devices for too long; they sometimes turn into a sort of soup, and everything has to be uprooted and replanted to form separate groups again. The same thing applies on a larger scale to a cluttered landscape, when it no longer makes visual sense. To see it more clearly, take a walk in it by moonlight. The predominant forms and structures will then appear, and you can remove extraneous detail by judicious use of a chainsaw. To eliminate unnecessary features in a similar way, seventeenth-century painters used a Claude glass—a technique in which they looked at a scene through a smoked glass to select only the parts that deserved to be painted.

If you are nearsighted, simply taking off your glasses is often enough to enable you to distinguish the essential. In winter, nature sometimes helps us by covering up all our mistakes with a layer of snow. Sometimes a raking light shows up significant relief that we might otherwise ignore. Seeing a familiar place under unusual lighting conditions will often give us the opportunity to discover its aesthetic potential.

Above: An early morning mist makes the different planes in the background of a landscape stand out as clear, distinct masses, whereas they would probably all be a uniform green in daylight. We can all experience this revelation in our gardens, even if they are small.

Right: We can gaze at our gardens in the moonlight, as in this period photograph with a handwritten dedication by Paul Valéry: *"Et la lune perfide élève son miroir, jusque dans le secret de la fontaine"* ("And the perfidious moon raises her mirror, even into the secret of the fountain").

Down at the daisy roots or reaching for the sky

As we tend to find it easier to look from side to side than up and down, we must find ways to make our eyes leave the ground.

It is in gardens made up of island beds that we may most easily observe the difference between a recently created flower bed containing only low plants, perennials, or annuals and a garden area where we can already see shrubs with some fine-looking vertical branches. To achieve a quick result, we just need to acquire (or be given) some shrubs or woody plants that are already well developed: bamboo, elder, conifers such as junipers, Japanese mahonias, lilac, Japanese maple, and the like. A little artistic pruning will highlight the melodic lines of their branches, which will make us look upward to follow the design with our eyes.

The simple height of a shrub, even a common species such as forsythia, will draw our eyes upward when we look at a flower bed. (Les Colombages, Varengeville-sur-Mer)

Islands or islets

There are two ways to design a garden of island beds in a meadow. The first is to begin by laying out the beds, which then resemble islands, without paying any particular attention to the paths between them.

The second gives priority to the paths, whose fluid lines will guide walkers from one island to the next. In this case, the beds fill the gaps left by the paths. To lay out designs like this in a real situation, we

can use garden hoses to help visualize the contours we are looking for and to correct any flaws caused by optical effects related to undulations in the ground.

These lines generally create an impression of movement for the eyes, which then encourages us to put ourselves in motion to follow this movement. A pathway in the mind thus induces an actual pathway.

The magic of circles

Circles have a curious effect on our degree of concentration: the poetry of the concentric circles of raindrops on the surface of a pond, or the mysterious "crop signs" supposedly marked out in our fields by extraterrestrials. In general, circular clearings and the fairy rings of mushrooms we sometimes find in them, like anything round (wheels, Chinese doors and windows, the broad leaves of certain perennial plants), fascinate us. The circle, whether as a passageway or a dead end, whether as a visual fixation point or an imaginary line, will always deserve a prominent place in the garden.

The interplay of arches and circles serves to define a series of protective spaces. Drawings like these, by the brilliant architect Edwin Lutyens, can raise our spirits as though we were listening to a symphony. (Bois des Moutiers)

The circle often has a magical
connotation and can be used to stage
all kinds of garden effects of a more or
less sacred nature.

Above: The convex curves of fragrant plants on a sunny terrace at Hestercombe.

Left: Jardin Botanique in Nanterre.

Concave or convex lines

In nature, virtually all ground-cover plants tend to spread sideways, like the peripheral growth of clumps of bamboo or royal ferns. So it is by designing flower beds with convex, not concave, curves that we can give them a natural look.

The inverted arch is like a cup, offering the abundance of vegetation and opening to the unlimited space of the sky. (Bois des Moutiers)

Arches: Right way up or upside down

The use of different types of arches is evident in many famous gardens, including arched bridges reflected in water to form a perfect circle. Reversed arches are less common, yet very evocative. The English architect Edwin Lutyens used them as a symbolic element in the creation of his "dream house" at Bois des Moutiers (above). This form, which he had designed in stone or wood, was later echoed using clipped yew hedges. One can obtain similar effect by loosely stretching a chain between two pillars.

The merits of contrasting curved and broken lines

If the limits of a garden are curved, the dominant motifs inside these limits should be based on broken straight lines, and vice versa. Experience shows that adding circles to a curved space gives a closed-in feeling, and the same applies when adding broken straight lines to angular contours. In fact, it seems that diversity in design opens up the space and allows the observer to breathe. A similar idea applies to ways of dressing: would one wear a polka dot tie with a polka dot shirt, or a striped tie with a striped shirt?

Left: A sunken path gives the illusion that generations of walkers have taken ages to hollow it out. Bois des Moutiers

Below left: A winding stairway at Les Jardins de l'Albarède. (Created by S. Lapouge)

Opposite: Sunken pathway in the garden of Parham House (England). An ascending path is more visually interesting when it is winding, rather than straight.

Below right: Jardin de Valérianes.

Valleys, sunken gardens, stairways, terraces, stepped ramps

Judicious excavation can serve to convert a flat enclosure with all-too-obvious limits into a more interesting undulating terrain, with surprises and unexpected views that make the observer think the garden is much larger than it really is. When designed by a skilful artist-gardener, the contours of these changes of level can look even more beautiful in the deep shadows of early morning or late evening.

Creating hollowed-out paths in these scale-model landscapes gives the impression that they have been there for a very long time, like the paths we see in seventeenth-century landscape paintings.

Sometimes we get tired of flat gardens, however well decorated they may be with rich tapestries of plants, and we seek to introduce a dramatic element by digging out the ground to make a sunken garden (below right, Jardin de Valérianes, Normandy). Why are some of us so reluctant to take the downward plunge and dig out our gardens? Too many associations with deep, melancholy wells or even grave-diggers? In any case, if we go ahead, the creation of stairways and steps takes on a critical importance. They can be straight or curved, in successive layers, or twisting; the variety of shapes and materials is almost infinite, and they lend themselves to all sorts of contortions and distortions. All these stairways and slopes help us gain valuable space while lending rhythm to our steps.

Different types of stairs for the garden

Architects have always paid great attention to making their slopes as pleasant as possible. (See Blondel's 1675 formula in the Appendix, page 143.)

Stairways in all their forms are the key to any transition between different levels of consciousness.

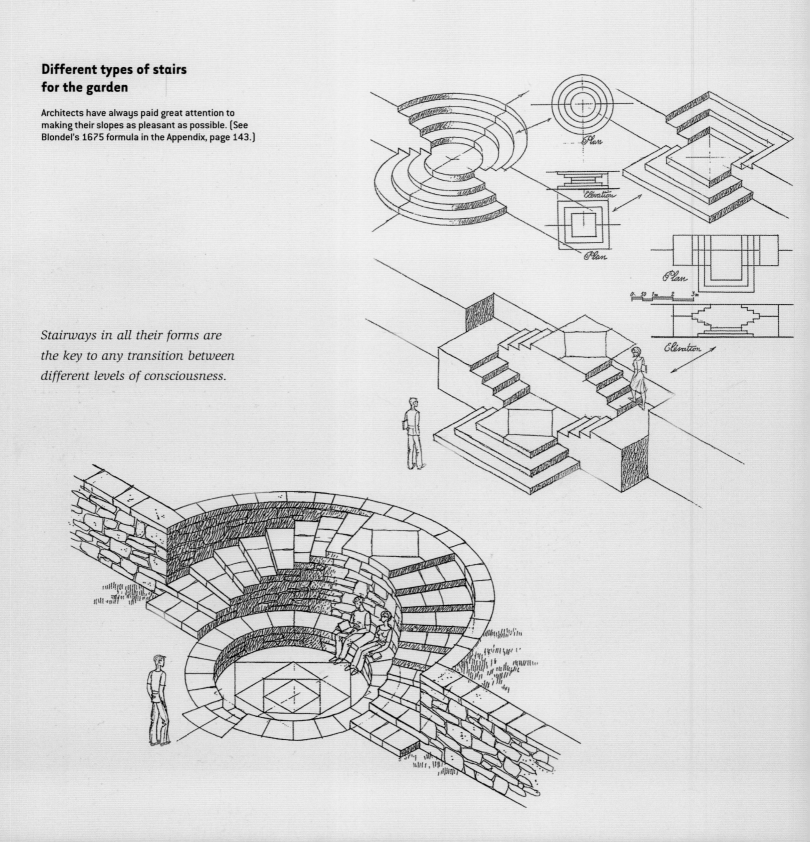

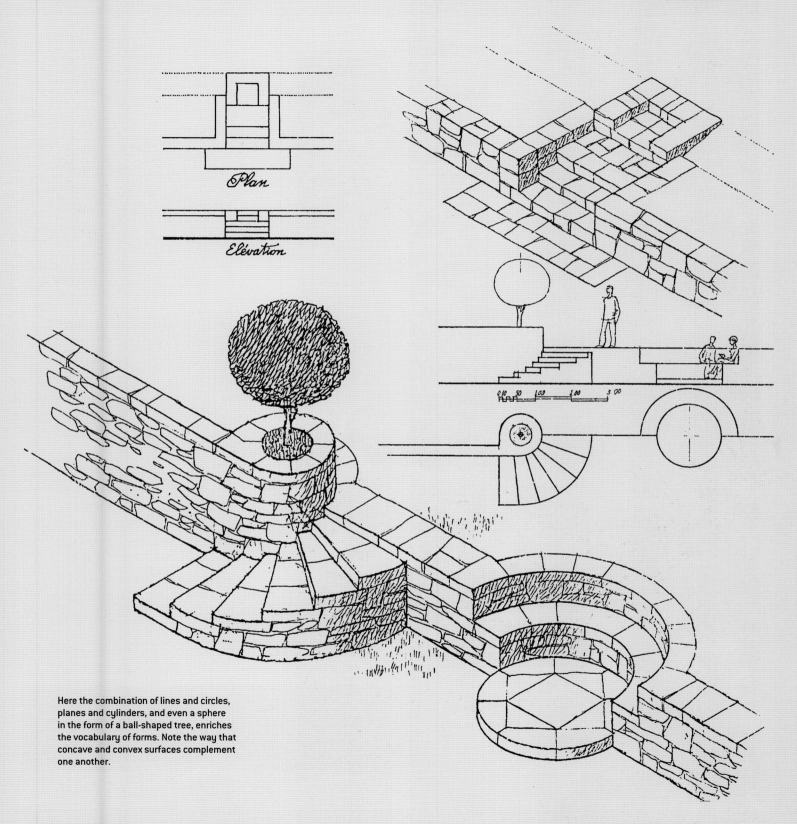

Plan

Élévation

Here the combination of lines and circles, planes and cylinders, and even a sphere in the form of a ball-shaped tree, enriches the vocabulary of forms. Note the way that concave and convex surfaces complement one another.

A vertical garden at the bottom of a courtyard. (Patrick Blanc's brilliant invention)

Gaining height: Embankments, rock gardens, vertical gardens

If excavating a garden creates space, we must not neglect other vertical resources to create new areas for planting. It is easy to erect embankments to mark the boundaries of a garden, and these will provide additional planting space.

The building of rockeries, so dear to the hearts of alpine plant lovers, is based on the same principle of increasing the garden's usable surface area, as is the building of raised beds surrounded by dry stone walls.

The vertical gardens, or living walls, conceived and executed with such skill by Patrick Blanc have enriched the vocabulary available to the creation of artistic gardens (photos at left).

On flat terrain, in addition to the opportunities offered by digging out and piling up the soil, the judicious placing of plants of different heights will lead observers' eyes upward, to the point of feeling that they themselves are levitating because they lose all sense of altitude.

The art of lopsidedness

By observing the stance of Classical statues, where the weight of the figure's body is shifted to one side, thereby creating two different curves, we see how the lopsided effect can also be applied to gardens. Putting the axis off-center symbolizes another frame of reference, a different viewpoint. This rule is often imposed in architecture; even when the lopsidedness is only slight, it tends to give more power to a composition. Feng shui gardens are based on the need to let energy (chi) flow, so they adopt this technique to avoid the straight line that leads to "leakage" of the power of attention. The shift in perspective, in contrast, energizes the view.

A sideways shift in the perspective of the pathway suggests another possible route, and thus other pleasant possibilities. (Jardin de Valérianes)

Open spaces, closed spaces, monastery gardens

Now let us consider the case of gardens that offer no escape outward: enclosed, and sometimes secret, as is often the case with city gardens. The rules of perspective then have to be applied in the opposite direction. The limits of the garden should be broken up by doubling them with alignments of more or less regular vertical structures. The overall effect is that the eye and mind, instead of being transported into the distance, are in some way turned inward, inclining the observer to meditation, introspection, and dreams.

There is still expansion in gardens like these, but toward an inner world. Objects of meditation are then placed in the center of the garden (embroidery-work parterres and fountains in medieval gardens, floral rugs and precious objects in Persian gardens, rocks in Zen gardens.)

Interior walls and floors can sometimes be decorated with different multicolored patterns. The fact is that to express a sense of the sacred and precious, human beings have always felt the need to reserve and enclose particular places: caves, chapels, temples, cathedrals, or walled gardens, which they have decorated with paintings, sculpture, stained glass, mosaics, or climbing plants.

Above left: The contrast of rhythmic masses, defensive on the outside (above left), protective on the inside (opposite), creates a space conducive to meditation. (Private garden, Ste. Marguerite-sur-Mer)

Left: This confined space, on a much reduced scale, becomes a place of great emotion, elated as it is by the discreet fountain and paving of small pebbles. (Created by Pascal Gasquet, Courson, spring 2003)

Plan by Louis Benech for a proposed arboretum at the Château de Bosmelet.

The spiral can be used in the creation of ponds and water features, as below. (Hampton Court, near London)

The singular sign of the spiral and the use of the helix

A spiral motif has been chosen for many gardens.

In general, this very ancient symbol works best when it is serves a guiding role. The observer's eye follows the pattern of the curve, but it is the mind and thoughts that move along the lines of the spiral. The most pleasing use is that of double, triple, or quadruple spirals that lead the eye first toward the center and then back again, from the center to the outside.

Conical helixes offer other possibilities. If we follow a path—not just in our thoughts this time, but with our feet—we may move toward a platform (for example, at the top of a hill to enjoy a beautiful view) and then go down again by a different path. In the Japanese Garden at the Albert Kahn Gardens in Boulogne-Billancourt (where the motif is used in a quasi-symbolic way, with shelly limestone paving), one can see a gaping hole in the shape of a dizzying spiral, where a thin trickle of water follows the spiral down to the bottom of the hole.

In comparison, the simple design of a spiral on pavement may seem rather ordinary, even boring. Note, however, the possibility of a mosaic design with two superimposed spirals going in opposite directions, inspired by the arrangement of seeds in sunflowers. This defies our vision: a physiological obstacle, forming part of our nature, prevents our minds from choosing which of the two spirals to retain; the result is that after some hesitation our sight becomes blurred.

Opposite: The double spiral of the sunflower and paving designs inspired by it, including the Piazza del Campidoglio in Rome, by Michelangelo.

The spiral and its derivatives

Spirals of the sunflower, and paving
derived from them

Piazza del Campidoglio in Rome, by Michelangelo

Paving: flagstones, "crazy pavings" and brick

An example of "crazy paving" (*opus incertum*), apparently chaotic yet preparing us for the emergence of a central geometric motif, a symbol of organized life. (Bois des Moutiers)

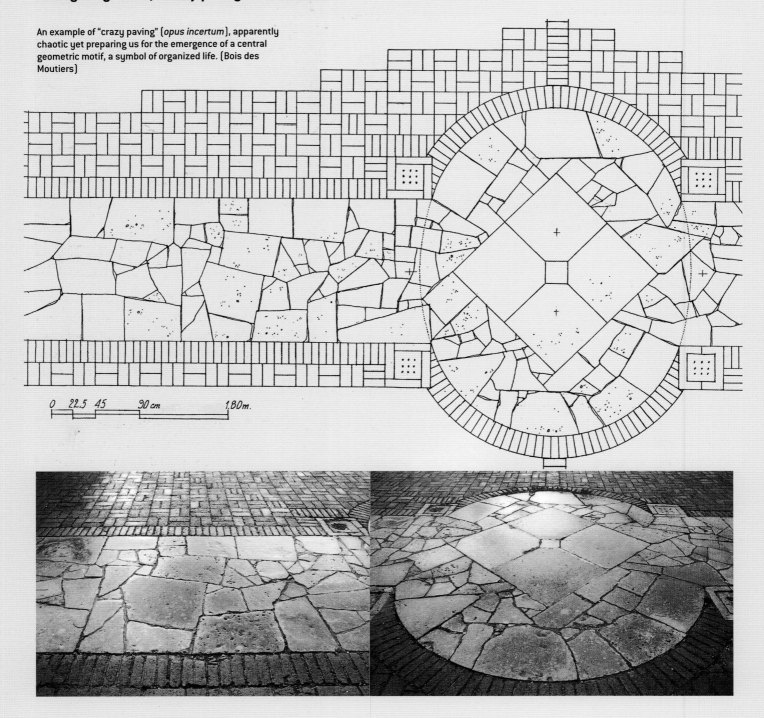

Regular or fragmented

The use of paving consisting of checkerboard patterns made up of polygons or repetitive forms provides geometric or rhythmic markers that our eyes enjoy recognizing. Regular patterns like this can also be distorted to deliberately lead our senses astray.

Equally amusing are the seemingly chaotic lines of randomly broken slabs: crazy paving, sometimes also called *opus incertum*. Here it is a question of choice between "a certain order" and "a certain chaos," between a clear order and a hidden one. We discern that the latter exists, but its mechanism is undetectable at first sight. It is characteristic of many Chinese or Japanese stone gardens, on which European landscape gardeners have drawn heavily.

We are usually only able to recognize things that fit in with mental categories we already have established, based on habit. Yet have we not all been gradually led into trying out new forms of art, painting, and music that, revolutionary in their time, have been rejected at first by proponents of a conservatism that is closed to all change? What now seems so difficult to understand may well seem only natural to us tomorrow.

Thus passing from easily recognizable forms to new forms of art, we are driven to expand our vision toward other dimensions and to measure ourselves in terms of worlds that are still unknown to us.

Stanley Kubrick's 1968 film *2001: A Space Odyssey* was a shock to many of those

Above: A checkerboard garden pattern that could readily lend itself to computer-aided distortion.

who saw it at the time. They said it made them suddenly change from one space age to another, for the price of a movie. On entering the cinema they knew that the earth is round and revolves around the sun, but they suddenly discovered that the moon is no longer a flat-looking light hanging in the sky and that a whole universe of other worlds in motion was hiding behind it, ever farther in the distance. This triggered something in their minds and opened their eyes.

Some rare individuals have an almost instinctive ability to create structures that are apparently irregular and yet pleasing to the eye. Are they gifted with a visual compass, or do they have a higher level of intelligence that enables them to identify all the possibilities of a design and to choose the most aesthetically pleasing ones more quickly than the rest of us? What some have naturally, others laboriously try to gain by

making many visits to well-designed gardens and also by observing nature, in order to train their visual memory. They sometimes resort to higher mathematics or use computers to help them.

"Special effects" gardens

Intricate checkerboards depicting the struggle between day and night, mazes designed to encourage meditation or introspection, spirals giving the illusion of movement. Yesterday it was Vasarely and other masters of kinetic art, and today it is experts using CAD software that can distort reality, who lead us ever farther into a modified perception of reality, which is after all the art of trompe l'oeil.

We may expect, for better or for worse, a revolution in garden design and the birth of a new style of special effects gardens whose design will be computer assisted.

Relative scale

*"For the foot can no more climb without
a ladder than the eye can without proportions."*

Paul Claudel

Changes and breaks in scale

When gardens look wrong, it is often because of mistakes in scale: a great big cedar tree in a small suburban garden, or a little rose-bush in the middle of a wide lawn. Yet we can make use of common errors of taste like these to create more space in a garden.

Abrupt transition from a reduced scale to larger scale creates a feeling of dizziness, making us lose all sense of real space to the advantage of an imaginary space that then seems larger than life. This is the effect we get with a footpath at the edge of a precipice, but also with the sight of a landscape viewed through a window divided into small leaded lights (photos below).

We may also observe, when looking at the grounds surrounding houses, that usually the best-kept parts are nearest to the house and that the space becomes wilder looking the farther we move away; the most remote parts are generally those needing the least maintenance. Thus smoothly tended lawns give way to well-mown grass farther away, then to meadows, and finally to undergrowth. This difference in the treatment of spaces is itself a variable dimension related to the amount of time needed to walk through them. By varying the proportions of each type of space, or by mixing them, we can create the illusion of more space.

The desire to change the scale of our usual surroundings is probably also the reason for our desire to travel and even to create gardens. Most of us live in an urban environment, in a world that is increasingly fixed and mineral (that is, comprising stone, concrete, and pavement), and we

Abrupt changes in the level of the tops of yew or beech hedges can accurately mark divisions and subdivisions of scale. (Great Dixter)

need to retrieve the sense of wonder that "plant cathedrals" can bring us. This is the opposite of the Middle Ages, when people made journeys through immense forests to discover, with amazement, stupendous cathedrals of stone decorated with glowing stained glass.

How to choose a scale; choice of the number of spaces

We have to make an important decision right at the beginning of the creation of a garden. Does it form part of a bigger site? What is its surface area in proportion to the total area we can see: a third, a fifth, a seventh? How

An opening in this wall of yew hints
at another garden beyond, arousing
our curiosity. (Great Dixter)

many parts can the garden itself be divided into: two, three, five, or seven parts? The more parts it is divided into, the less calm the final impression will be. But, for obvious reasons, too low a number will limit the possibilities of creating an illusion of space.

Once we have noted the garden's proportion in relation to its site (e.g., one-quarter), it is also a good idea to mark out (or modulate) each part of the garden in identical ratios (in this example, four). This gives a harmonious and coherent "music" to the whole, composed of "half notes" and "quarter notes" and even, going farther into the details, "eighth notes" or "sixteenth notes," without being too rigid about all this.

A garden of rooms

Each separate space provides an opportunity to focus the observer's attention. This is the principle of the "garden of rooms," and it offers a great many possibilities to the owner of a plot of virgin land. Specialized gardening journals often publish plans for such creations. Beyond the fact that dividing the garden into a number of rooms makes you think that its total area is bigger than it really is, choosing different themes for each room can yield a variety of impressions conducive to escape and relaxation. This type of garden also stimulates curiosity, leading to a series of surprises.

A garden made up of intercommunicating rooms provides a fine opportunity for children to play hide and seek.

Gardens of rooms

Symmetrical and centered plan

A central, circular chamber with four rooms of identical shape leading off from it; these rooms may, however, gain very different aspects by means of the plant and mineral materials used within each one.

Free plan

Here the space is more fluid, with the spiral shape of the hedge defining a space that is almost completely closed in, thus creating the effect of a den. A tree could also be planted to provide shade.

Top: Changes in scale can create an optical effect that has, so far, been little used in small gardens. (Private garden, Iclon, Normandy)

Bottom: Compositions made up from very small leaves can open our eyes to a wider world on a much reduced scale. (Private garden, Iclon, Normandy)

Elasticity of mental markers; bonsai gardens

Our brains are constituted in such a way that from one moment to the next they are perfectly capable of carrying us from a very large space to a much smaller one: like Alice in Wonderland, we can shrink in our imagination. So the little girl from the housing project who puts her rubber boots on and goes out to sit beside a thin trickle of water flowing from a fountain in the local park may very well close her eyes and, in her thoughts, find herself by the sea, where she dreams of being.

The vogue for miniature gardens installed in troughs or granite basins has been inspired by the ideas behind Japanese or Chinese bonsai gardens. This representation on a smaller scale of a much larger natural world is intended to liberate us from our everyday environment and to allow us to escape into an idealized world. It can even serve as a real therapy for people who are trapped inside their own mental universe.

Today we can find all sorts of miniature and slow-growing plants that, when planted in raised beds, can give to those who only have very small spaces the opportunity to create much larger, dreamlike spaces.

Left: A trompe l'oeil scene, increasingly common in cities, whose use could easily be extended to small gardens. (Created by Patricia Lemaigre-Dubreuil)

Below: Growing plants in pots, and bedding-in these plants outside in the garden, are practices derived from the art of interior flower arranging. (Bertrand Laffillé's garden in Varengeville-sur-Mer)

approach, we have seen theater backdrops employed to hide unsightly corners of the garden. Trompe l'oeil painting can serve to decorate the garden with false balustrades or with doors and windows that open onto other, imaginary spaces.

In the eighteenth century, Carmontelle invented "landscape transparencies": long, transparent paintings portraying, for example, the changing seasons, which slowly unrolled in front of the spectators. The development of *son et lumière* nighttime entertainments, and the increasingly frequent use of light shows projected onto the walls of historic cities or the facades of cathedrals, also present a wide field of creative possibilities for enlivening our gardens at night. Virtual imaging techniques provide the means to create impalpable and moving images and have created a demand for totally unexpected, continuously evolving theatrical happenings—such as a palm tree that grows to full height in a week, or colors that change in intensity depending on the time of day. Add to this a couple of erupting volcanoes, two or three holograms of dinosaurs, and we end up with a domestic Disneyland or, even worse, a mini Las Vegas! However, speaking

Trompe l'oeil: Illusions and staged effects

If the techniques used to create illusions on theater sets and, even more so today, in television studios are applied to the garden, then a wide field of possibilities opens up. The ones most frequently employed use trompe l'oeil images, of the sort that we often see painted on gable walls in city streets. These were once reserved for interiors, but why not use them in the garden to hide or disguise party walls?

If the wall at the back of a courtyard is painted blue, it can give the illusion of a view of the sea in the distance. Painting like this features two parts: a lighter blue for the sky, a darker blue for the sea. In a more radical

of crazy extravagance, haven't we already seen grandiose achievements—very real this time, not virtual—such as the *grandes eaux* at Versailles or the extraordinary creations at Wörlitz? The modification of scenic elements of the garden by remote control is now within everyone's reach, with signs that change angles, views that open or close, levels that drop or rise. As of now, the theater is entering our gardens.

On a more down-to-earth level, we may have dreams of wonderful plant associations that clash with reality, when plants do not bloom in the same season. To make our dreams come true, we can use the horticultural technique of bedding-in: i.e., forcing exotic plants to flower out of season in the greenhouse and then surreptitiously sneaking them into the flower beds. Visitors then will not believe their eyes. The return to reality involves risks and constraints. But are not these limitations just the circumstances that foster our creativity? In this way, the gardener becomes a stage director.

Example of bedding-in: this artificially forced chrysanthemum has been placed in a garden where grasses, sagebrush, and lamb's ear *(Stachys lanata)* are in season. (Denmans, created by John Brookes)

Mirrors and reflections: Buying a corner of heaven

Mirrors provide a powerful means to expand our visual space. The technique has been used for a long time in many gardens (e.g., the stairs of the Villa d'Este and the Chinese pavilion at the Bois des Moutiers). The rule is to always place the mirror at 45 degrees to the direction that observers are facing. They will discover another garden reflected in this mirror (a reflection of the one facing them), but they will not be able to see themselves; in fact, they run a serious risk of crashing into the mirror! In spite of this, the mirror does provide a large additional area requiring no maintenance at all (illustration on page 48). However, we should be aware of the fire risk that a mirror with an irregular surface can cause.

If the mirror is tilted slightly upward it introduces a new element borrowed from the sky, again without observers being able to see themselves in it (illustration on next page 49). Smaller mirrors may also be used, hidden in the bushes or strategically placed in unexpected locations, to create entertaining effects (this page, left.)

One can also obtain dramatic expansion of the garden by constructing a pond or canal, located so that the viewing angle is smaller than the angle of incidence; thus, the surface water reflects the sky. This provides infinitely rich opportunities to marvel at the sight of constantly changing views, with drifting clouds and migrating birds, not to mention the interest that aquatic fauna or flora can bring (see above and opposite page.)

By implementing a particularly skillful design, it is possible to devise a system where the image of a mirror is reflected in the water and the mirror itself reflects a part of the sky.

The effect of reflection in the water of

Above: In a tiny city garden, carefully placed mirrors make the boundaries disappear. (The Greenhouse, Chertsey, England)

Above right: The Alchemist's Garden. (Created by Maurière and Ossart)

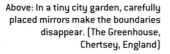

A pool without coping demonstrates what the mirror effect can add to an otherwise unremarkable landscape. (Jardin Plume, created by S. and P. Quibel)

a pond can be enhanced by building it so that viewers do not notice the coping around the edges, which are located beyond their field of vision.

Remembering reflections of the sky seen from a hilltop or cliff overlooking a lake or calm sea, or even wet sand (such being the famous view of the cliffs at Varengeville-sur-Mer painted by Claude Monet), we may note that a mere puddle in the garden, even if it is very shallow, can produce this sought-after mirror effect. It can even serve for observing gorgons in your garden without being turned to stone, should the occasion arise!

A floor made of a reflective surface (marble or polished granite) can give the altogether pleasant illusion of walking on transparent water. Facing an evenly lit ceiling (which eliminates the "cave effect" of traditional lighting) this "mirror floor" can bring a real sense of liberation, a kind of refreshing weightlessness. In general, the mirror abolishes obstacles, removes any sense of claustrophobia, and frees the mind as if by magic.

Faithful mirror

A mirror at right angles to the direction of the path reflects the walkers' image back at them—as well as that of the pergola, which thus visually doubles in length. It is also possible to place the mirror not at right angles, but at 45 degrees to the axis of the pergola. This "misleading" mirror then reflects the image of what is on the right in the drawing, extending the visual space.

Section

Toward the reflected sun

Reflection of the shadows of the pillars

Mirror

Toward the sun

Plan

Misleading mirror

Here the mirror is slightly tilted upward; it does not reflect the viewer's image, but that of part of the sky, creating the illusion of pushing the boundaries of the garden outward toward infinity.

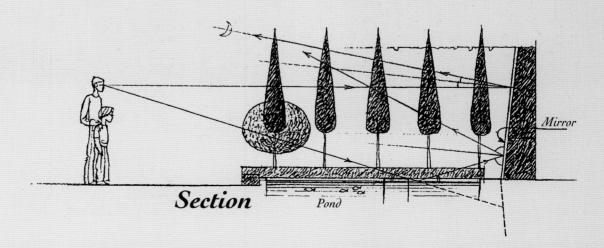

Mirror

Section   *Pond*

A light mist can make us lose all notion of depth. The landscape becomes a canvas painted in silhouette. (Jardin Plume)

reveal a totally different view of the reflection we usually see.

A blurred image produces, by analogy, the illusion of distance. Perception of an unreal world makes us wonder about where we are ourselves. Should we get closer to see it more clearly? Are we ourselves blurred, for someone observing us from a distance? In this case, could there be another world more real than ours?

Mist and fog make us lose all sense of distance; they make our natural focusing mechanism go wild. When we reach a certain level of being unable to see things properly, fear takes over from what, just before, was still just a question of concentration. Our curiosity about the unknown and our desire to go beyond give way to uncertainty and disorientation. We should therefore, perhaps, take particular care when using blurred images in the garden.

Moving mist, which makes a landscape first appear and then disappear, creates something like a natural game of hide and seek.

In the same vein, our brain naturally joins up dotted lines; but when these lines are partially erased, they can be read in different ways and open up possibilities to our imagination. This kind of game, which already exists in graphic art, does not yet seem to have found a use in gardens.

Having fun looking for the shape of a face or an animal in clouds, rock formations, or stones is a pastime that develops the sense of observation. Less fugitive than clouds, funny-looking pebbles also have their place in the garden.

Blurred images, stippled images, erased lines

Images that are deliberately blurred or partially erased have an aesthetic value of their own; painters and photographers, for example, have used technique to suggest the idea of movement. The Impressionists in particular found that it enabled them to make their paintings more vivid, shimmering, and vibrant. In the garden, a light breath of air over the surface of a pond can suddenly

Projected shadows and spots of light

Plants with different leaf forms, placed so that light coming from the side projects their shadows on a wall or some other even surface, have not been used very much as a method of enlarging the space (e.g., the projection of bamboo on a white wall).

A similar method could involve the projection of spots of light using, for example, pieces of colored glass set in open metalwork. Mounted together with a few pieces of irregularly shaped mirror in the form of a mobile and moved by the wind, they can be very useful in enlivening the corner of a courtyard or city garden.

Shadows that disturb

Like lights, shadows play a crucial role in gardens, constantly changing our perception of scale. Imagine, for example, on a winter morning, looking at a ten-foot-high shrub located on the east side of the garden. Its shadow, multiplied sixty times by the winter sun, will be three hundred yards long, crossing the garden and perhaps going beyond it to annoy the next-door neighbor!

Bearing in mind that the sun is lower on the horizon during the winter months, we must carefully choose the location of trees and shrubs so as to avoid casting unwelcome shadows.

Hedges in particular require special attention. If they are too dense and south-facing, they will create deep shade on the other side that few plants will appreciate. It is possible to make openings in them, sometimes even at the base, so that rays of light can penetrate to the darkest areas.

Making use of the adjoining landscape

By arranging for the garden to have a view of a particular building or part of the landscape outside the garden's boundaries (a church tower, a wooded hill, or a wide valley), the owner appropriates the beauty of the surrounding site, perhaps obeying some law that states that a landscape belongs to the person who looks at it.

It can even be interesting to draw inspiration from the landscape outside the

At the Parc André Malraux in Nanterre, the landscape architect Jacques Sgard manages to make us forget the oppressive environment of the skyscrapers of La Défense by placing his garden in the hollow of an artificial crater.

The smallest picturesque element in the surrounding landscape can be used skillfully to create beautiful views from the garden. (The Garden House)

garden to compose the inside, creating the illusion that the inside is only a continuation of the much larger space surrounding it. This is one of the guiding principles of Zen gardens.

Like Prince Andrei in Tolstoy's novel *War and Peace*, who, wounded and lying on his back, discovers the beauty of the sky, we too can create places of observation where we can contemplate the beauties of the sky by day: the dance of the clouds and glorious rays of light. At night, gazing at the stars makes us conscious not only of how small we are, but also of what a privilege it is to exist.

In Nanterre, the landscape architect Jacques Sgard created two hills: one in the shape of a truncated cone intended for just this kind of observation; the other, cone shaped but hollow at the center like a volcano crater, containing a botanical garden. In this garden you can forget about the giant buildings surrounding the park, which are hidden by the sides of the crater (opposite, bottom).

Once again, you lose all sense of scale.

Distance

"The nearness counted so as distance."

Henry James (The Lesson of the Master, 1892)

"Only he who walks the road on foot learns of the power it commands, and of how . . . it calls forth distances, belvederes, clearings, and prospects at each of its turns like a commander deploying soldiers at a front."

Walter Benjamin (Einbahnstraße [One Way Street], 1928)

"Everything is a question of point of view."

Sir Edwin Lutyens

Applied perspective

The art of perspective created a revolution in the history of art. Today, if we apply our knowledge of these laws to gardens, it can significantly alter how we assess distance and visual space.

Our eyes are eager to search for vanishing points, and they delight in finding an open space rich in possibilities for escape, a site receding out of sight. How can we create the illusion of these open spaces when there is only a small space available to us? We can do this by leading the eye as far away as possible and by hinting at other openings still farther away. To help us, there are a number of devices we can use, which will be developed in the following pages:

- Making a series of objects seem ever more distant by artificially reducing their height.
- Gradually reducing the distance between trees in straight rows, following a geometrical sequence.
- Increasing the number of bends in a winding path.
- Lengthening the appearance of a pathway by exaggerating the way it appears to become narrower in the distance.
- Hollowing out or increasing the natural hollow of a valley.

If, when our eyes search for distant objects and scenes, the image that our brain perceives is based on false references, we lose all sense of exact distances.

We must take care, however, to avoid introducing a decorative element into the overall design (like a bench or statue) outside the proportions specified in the particular context of our artificial perspective, because this would immediately destroy the illusion we are seeking.

An apparent dead end will make the viewer's eyes go off in search of a vanishing point, and if they do not find it, they will end up going around in circles. But as long as the apparent movement around the scene is easy, our mind will not feel confined and we will accept what our eyes see.

Different methods of visually lengthening distance

❧ Making a series of objects seem ever more distant by artificially reducing their height

Here the height of each tree is successively reduced by 20 cm (8 in). To make the effect even more credible, the width of the path should also be reduced.

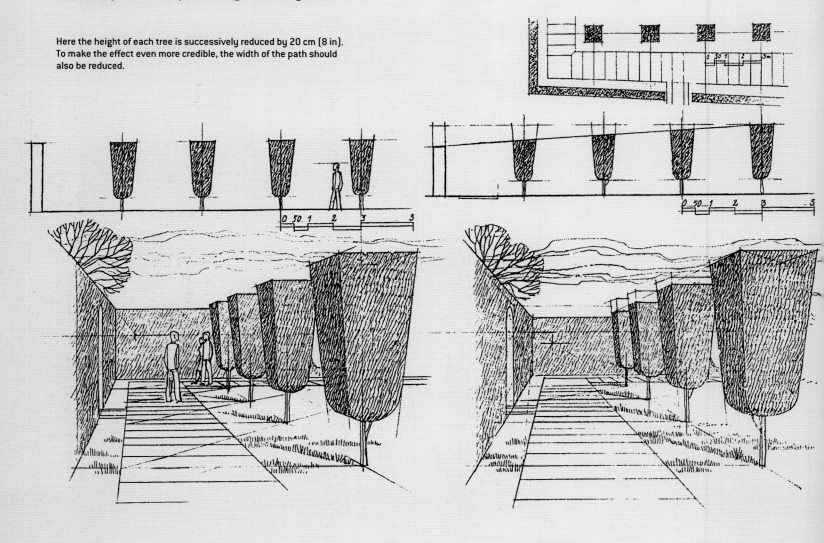

❈ Gradually reducing the distance between trees in straight rows

As the first gap between the trees is 3 m (10 ft), the observer, assuming them equal to one another, will instinctively assume that the sixth tree is 15 m (50 ft) away, whereas in fact the distance is only 12 m (39 ft).

✴ Increasing the number of bends in a winding path

A winding path, rather than a straight one, can artificially extend the space (see also page 14).

✴ Lengthening the appearance of a pathway by exaggerating the way it appears to become narrower in the distance

(Hampton Court, 2003)

Hollowing out or increasing the natural hollow of a valley

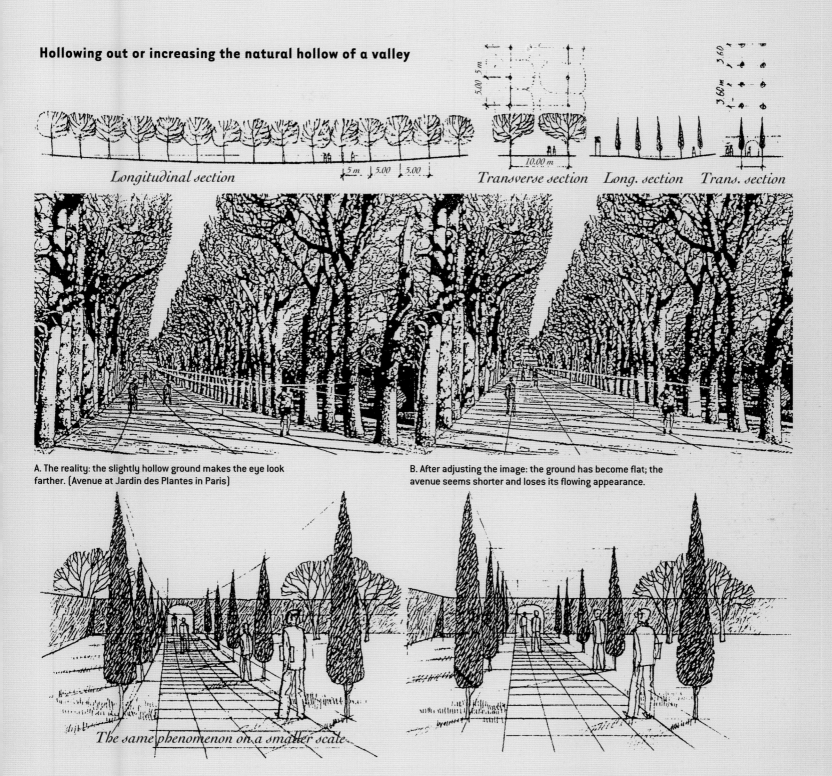

Longitudinal section   5 m | 5.00 | 5.00

5.00 5 m

Transverse section   10.00 m   *Long. section*   *Trans. section*

3.60 3.60

3.60 m

A. The reality: the slightly hollow ground makes the eye look farther. (Avenue at Jardin des Plantes in Paris)

B. After adjusting the image: the ground has become flat; the avenue seems shorter and loses its flowing appearance.

The same phenomenon on a smaller scale.

The contrast between a closely planted area and a clearer space beyond it evokes a feeling of liberation and a restful vision for our eyes. (Jardin Plume, created by S. and P. Quibel)

Visual "traps"

Some gardens just make us bored. A lack of structure or of design altogether gives a tiring impression of disorganization, like an ill-conceived museum where objects are piled up in no apparent order. Other gardens, in contrast, refresh us; we come out of them feeling happy and full of energy. The fact is that consciously or not, we have been "trapped"—led on by a successive chain of pleasant views designed to attract our eyes and stimulate our attention. In this way perspectives, whether true or false, arouse in us a desire to move forward. Fleeting views

This doorway gives us a glimpse of a whole world waiting to be discovered. (Jardin du Grand Courtoiseau)

through tree trunks or branches make us guess at wonderful things waiting to be discovered beyond. Overhanging spaces produce a fascination with the emptiness below and a dizziness that awakens our senses. In most cases, the subtle interplay of distances and proportions draws our attention to charm us all the more.

Trellises and false perspectives

Trellises of all kinds are now available at garden centers; by no means all of them are designed as trompe l'oeil! When ordering them it is important to make sure that the optimal distance for viewing them is clearly indicated, along with their dimensions.

A succession of planes seen in exaggerated perspective (doors, trimmed hedges, columns) will produce an effect of space that can be doubled by setting up a mirror in front of it.

Doors, windows, gratings, screens, latticework

Doors and windows created either in architecture or in nature are among the most common visual traps. They can take the form of different types of openings in mineral or vegetable walls (photo opposite and following pages). We can sometimes

discover them occurring naturally in a mass of greenery and then fix them in place, just for fun (photo above). It is also a well known fact that the edges of a frame focus our attention on the image contained with in it, sharpening and giving power to our vision. This "telescope" effect (or "microscope"; in any case, it seems to bring the observed object closer to the observer) lends itself to multiple uses. We think here of grids, gratings, and small-paned windows. (Indeed,

Unforeseen or arranged openings in garden settings. Opposite, top: at Bois des Moutiers; above: at The Garden House, an opening in a *Camellia sasanqua*.

Opposite, bottom: A grid whose pattern can be read in two different ways (left), and a bamboo mesh window (right, Les Jardins d'Ombre et Lumière, Courson, spring 2003).

looking at a landscape through a small window pane and drawing it with a little piece of soap directly on the glass is practically the definition of perspective). An interesting alternative, which can introduce variation into the way we look at what lies beyond the frame, is to choose, as a framework to look through, a grid whose pattern can be read in two different ways. Lattice screens, of the type found in traditional Arabian houses, bring rays of light into a shaded or enclosed space; they also enable characters in novels to observe the street or the neighborhood without being seen.

Belvederes, gazebos, watchtowers

Pavilions of this kind would sometimes be located on the corners of estates surrounded by walls, and they were used to survey the surrounding countryside. We, the heirs of the watchmen who perched on top of medieval towers, can look out to experience panoramic

views that take us beyond our enclosed universe. What a way to see beautiful views this is; at times, it is also useful to foresee tomorrow's weather.

Distance and light

A remarkable object in the garden, the one that will most successfully attract our eyes, depends not only on its more or less privileged position, nor on how well lit it may be, but also on where we find ourselves in relation to it. Whether it is in the limelight or entirely in the shade, our appreciation of it will depend on these two variables: lighting and distance.

In the case of low light intensity, we will get closer to the object to see it better. Therefore, it is possible to make it seem closer or more distant by placing it more or less in the light. We shall see, however, that

Depending on where they are situated, some plants can be so transformed by their "suit of lights" that we hardly recognize them.

this is not the case with all objects, which can look nearer or farther away depending on their value (light or dark) and also on their hue (i.e., where they fall in the color spectrum) and even on whether they are being viewed by men or women (it seems this is the case for the color red)! By playing on the position of objects and choosing to light them up or not, we can create the impression of a larger space.

These amazing properties can be put to use in both internal and external decoration. A vase of flowers, lit in a certain way and placed within reach on a nearby table, invites us to plunge our face into it to smell its fragrance. In the garden at night, the mistress

or master of the house, using a remote control as if it were a magic wand, can light up any element of the decor, whether it is a "folly" or some other garden feature or a particular flowering shrub.

By day, the choice of the angle of natural light (different for each plant), depending on whether it is morning or evening, can either bring out or efface any chosen element of the garden depending on the season or the time of day.

Thus the foliage of holly looks matte black or glossy white depending on whether it is lit straight on or sideways. Witch hazels in February need to be lit from the side for the flowers' quality to be fully revealed. Azaleas in

The fashion for ornamental grasses
gives possibilities for soft lighting effects
that capture their light, downy textures.
(Old Vicarage, Norfolk, England)

Left, top: The beauty of grasses is enhanced when the light passes through them. (Old Vicarage)

Left, bottom: The famous tree peony *P. rockii* only fully reveals its dazzling white when seen against the morning light.

it look sublime, with a beauty that becomes immediately obvious regardless of whether the viewer has any prior botanical knowledge. A path that leads right up close to a back-lit plant allows us to fully appreciate its beauty and delicacy of texture. We have seen a five-year-old child from an underprivileged background standing in front of a bush that was glistening with light, crying out to other children of his age, "Look, look, it's beautiful!" "It's more than beautiful!" added another child.

In praise of shadows

If glare can dazzle us and make us go temporarily blind, then shadows, in contrast, increase our visual capacity, which gains in breadth what it loses in sharpness as it puts all the receptor cells of the eye into play. Thus we see our gardens in a whole new way at dusk during extended summer evenings out on the terrace. Those who are fortunate enough to have an area of woodland in their garden can make a shaded pathway through it that will provide coolness and rest for the eyes in the height of the summer heat. But to make out the fine details of flowers, we need to get up close to them because our capacity for image resolution diminishes with the level of illumination.

the spring look their best when seen against the light. Each plant has its own optimum lighting conditions. Candles mounted on the backs of tortoises gave, it seems, the ideal light to admire tulips at the time of their first glory in the seventeenth century—the very same light that suits women's complexions so well! The setting sun sublimates the red of red camellias, rendering them still more sublime.

Front lighting or back lighting

If you are a garden photographer or even someone who makes television documentaries about gardens, you can count on back lighting to guarantee the "oohs and ahs." If direct sunlight can efface the beauty of a plant, then lighting it from behind can make

Under the last rays of evening light, plants take on a particular aspect: a brightness due to the special quality of light, then a sparkling aspect due to the fact that the eye is less able to distinguish the contours. The quality of the air also contributes to this phenomenon.

Planting distances

This is a frequent problem facing any beginner in the art of landscape: how to arrange a certain number of trees or shrubs so that they look natural (if this is indeed the desired effect). A group of trees planted at irregular intervals gives a feeling of much larger space than would be the case if they were simply arranged at equal distances. There is a method that everyone can use, derived from the French dice game 421.

Surprisingly, the eye is quickly able to recognize the most visually satisfying intervals among points thrown at random on a sheet of paper. By throwing a number of dice equal to the number of subjects to be planted, we obtain via successive throws numerous possibilities of different proportions, renewed each time we throw, from which we can choose to retain only those that are pleasing to the eye. This can take place either directly on the ground with light objects or on paper first, which can then be transferred to the ground once we have chosen the arrangement.

In general, we avoid straight lines that pass through three or more plants (or points). Concerning the number of plants themselves, it is recommended to retain only odd or prime numbers (3, 5, 7 . . .). Experience shows that the greater the number of plants you have, the more risk there is of losing at least one. Unless you keep some plants in reserve in the nursery, it seems prudent to aim for an even number greater than the desired number, even if it means removing a plant later if all of them survive.

Tight planting—massed planting—simplifying the design

We should combat the current trend for planting trees at equal distances and trying to make every plant a park tree. We would do better to copy Mother Nature, who could not care less about our intellectual plots and plans. We should plant clumps of trees—groves and woods—and keep majestic specimen trees just for prime locations.

In a bed of perennials or annuals, it is better to mass plants together than to scatter them. Flat areas of textures or colors will

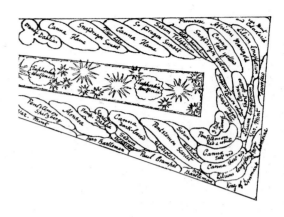

The technique of planting in long strips, as practiced by Gertrude Jekyll and since then by many other garden designers, gives depth to the masses of flowers. (Above, drawing by G. Jekyll; below, flower bed at Great Dixter)

Above: The giant leaves of the gunnera mark the boundary of this space, defining an area where one can have a well-earned rest after a day's hard work. (Deléris garden, Varengeville-sur-Mer, Normandy)

Opposite: Patches of light punctuate the pathway; visitors feel reassured because they can guess the direction intended for the visit. (Jardin de Valérianes, Normandy)

strengthen each of the selected elements. Planting at an angle to the path, as Gertrude Jekyll did, will give an illusion of depth where in fact there is only a thin strip of plants, because the strip is viewed end-on (see illustration).

Too many visual signals in a garden confuse its meaning, in the same way that a profusion of billboards at the entrance to a town puts us off reading any of them. Instead, we should try to find diversity by making use of the seasons, with one area or spot of color taking the place of the next one, with perennials succeeding bulbs, which are then replaced by other late perennials or summer bulbs.

Erasing boundaries

Magicians rarely reveal their secrets. Even if the magical effect found in a garden is the product of certain procedures, it should never be too obvious what the trick is.

So to make it more difficult to estimate the distance that separates us from the boundaries of a garden, all we have to do is erase those boundaries. Anything can be used to help: curtains of plants with small evergreen leaves; vaporous-looking shrubs capable of forming a kind of smoke screen; mirrors; even painted canvas. And, in contrast, we should never have hedges of the same species in a straight line or climbing plants with large leaves: these are real prison bars that generate a sense of depressing confinement. We should move the limits of our space as far away as we possibly can.

Curious proposals

When you can no longer see the outer limits of a space, you are no longer able to mentally focus on its interior details.

When you cannot see the interior details, you are not in a suitable frame of mind to look for the outer limits.

The first part of this observation explains why people visiting a public garden for the first time often want to know how big it is.

A space that is too large requires easily recognized borders. (Could this be the reason for the existence of such monuments as the Eiffel Tower and Montmartre in Paris, and the Berlin Funkturm?) By allowing us to transfer our attention to what is at our feet, such visual markers become a potent factor of liberation, a means of escape, a door open to dreams. In the words of the Christian mystic Karlfried Graf von Dürckheim, "[some places offer] plenitude, far from the multitude." Peace, contained within secure borders.

Different is the sense of worry in those who fruitlessly try to find their way among the trees that "hide the forest"; those who cannot imagine the limits since they have no immediate reference from which to build a route. This is probably what motivates Tom Thumb in the fairy tale to mark his way back with white pebbles, and what leads our Swiss

Cascades and small waterfalls are now available for all budgets. They are an incomparable source of relaxation. (Jardin d'Angélique, Normandy)

friends to say to people asking their way, "When you don't know, you don't go!" As in life, the absence of a plan of action produces anxiety, unless you have blind faith!

Once we have mentally fixed an object's position, we use our visual acuity to observe surrounding objects. Waltzers or trapeze artists acquire a fixed reference point amid the crowd of spectators, and this tells them

how to move in space. After recognizing the line of the road, the walker can boldly set off into the great forest. In this way, the boundaries of the garden are estimated and anticipated without fear.

More specifically, the reassuring presence of handrails or low walls along the edges of large terraces gives the visitor the freedom to look at the plantings down below, as well as the panorama beyond, with a sense of total security.

The importance of punctuation and its rhythm

All kinds of rhythms can be imprinted into the design of a garden. They can be obtained by a succession of objects, splashes of color, or different marks designed to retain the eye repeatedly and sometimes without the viewer's knowledge.

Thus we find steps, tree trunks or upright stones, rocks, bushes, sequences of light or brightly colored patches, clearings, ponds, and so on all being used in this way.

Just as in music when we perceive sequences of long sounds (half notes) or short sounds (quarter and eighth notes), the message given by the rhythm speaks immediately to our senses: large peaceful spaces or else disorder and din, a succession of circles and lines in a dance that may be either stately and regular or frenzied and delusional. An accelerating rhythm can play a useful role in elongating the perspective (according to the principle illustrated on page 57). In a large garden, dark corridors that encourage peacefulness may follow luminous clearings that inspire sudden wonder (photo on page 71). It is also said about public gardens that when walking around, visitors should get a "shock of beauty" every five minutes. In the present age of zapping, this requirement becomes even more compelling.

When the brain gets involved

Stare at the flames of a wood fire in the fireplace, or watch television with the sound turned off. We now know that when the brain is partially "disconnected," it emits waves of a different type from those that it emits when we engage in an intellectual activity.

The crystal ball that used to be found in some offices was not intended to see into the future, but to rest the eyes. Computer monitors with screen saver software can have a similar hypnotic effect.

It is, therefore, a good idea to reserve a corner of the garden as a rest area, with the special property of providing repose after the hard toil of the day. To this purpose one could, for example, install a fountain that squirts and spurts in a way that is unpredictable but always renewed; or a powerful waterfall that either boils over or flows delicately, according to the means available and the possibilities of the place; or else a place to enjoy watching the waters of a river, such as a footbridge.

All this takes us a long way away from the edicts of some office interior designers, which are slavishly followed by personnel directors who are no less ignorant of these issues and who, searching for unnecessary order, recommend that nothing appear on office walls or tables. We must instead allow and encourage people working in offices to line their walls with all sorts of images designed to give them pleasant and restful things to look at. For example, photographic enlargements covering all or part of a wall will transform the workplace into a veritable office landscape. A mixture of indoor plants of different species can also give people a way to rest their eyes for a moment before going back to their work.

In squalid or chaotic urban conditions, the development of "windows" looking out onto small, perfectly composed scenes can

Scene of harmony in urban Japan

The keep of Sissinghurst Castle provides a view looking down over the White Garden, thereby doubling its effect.

Any opportunity for looking down on a garden allows you to see in a whole new light.

provide the disoriented city-dweller with the opportunity to sit for a moment and regain some psychic strength by contemplating this harmonious vision. This method is commonly used in Japan (photo, right). Ideally, the whole city should become a work of art. This was once the case for the city of Rome, and even partly for Paris. But what will our descendants say about the disorderly architectural structures of our last century?

Quality of vision and visual memory

The role of the brain is involved in almost all the known stages of the development of vision:

❀ within the eye itself, vision is preliminarily filtered by a cerebral analysis of raw data;

❀ within the brain, a complex processing of data in several steps leads to the activation of different types of behavior.

It becomes clear that the quality of vision depends largely on visual memory, a kind of shared culture common to us all, which probably distinguishes humans from animals in both quantity and quality. Today there is not much room for visual memory in educational programs. Saint-Exupery's Little Prince would be very surprised to see what typical graduates of France's *grandes écoles* come up with when asked to "Draw me a garden"! But to create a successful garden it is not enough to have dreamed about it. The designer must have visually memorized scenes or plants admired in other gardens and then assembled them in a new, harmonious whole. The obstacles or possibilities that the designer encounters when applying them to a new place are an additional stimulus to creativity.

Tree houses, viewpoints, lookout towers

To completely renew the way you see your garden, there is an effective method: that of climbing trees. The attractions of views from above are well known by cats . . . and children; such views bring them a sense of security and superiority over the rest of the world. Detached from mankind's useless agitation, many cannot resist the urge to settle in more comfortably by building tree houses. "The Baron in the trees," eponymous hero of Italo Calvino's novel, even made one his permanent residence. When we compose patterns of elaborate parterres, we must remember that they will only be visible in their entirety from the upper floors of the house. This form of garden art developed in the seventeenth century from the time the main reception rooms left the ground floor to be installed on the "noble" floor upstairs. At Sissinghurst, you can observe the White Garden from the top of a tower.

Marked trails and guided visits

Like King Louis XIV personally conducting a tour of the Park of Versailles, the gardener will lead friends from one perfect view to another carefully chosen viewpoint. The choice of these prime locations is the result of reflection taking into account all the possibilities of the site: looking straight down, diagonally, framed, panoramic, and so on.

The design of a garden should be organized starting out from this original conception.

It is said that the young architect Edwin Lutyens, when called to speak before members of the Royal Institute of British Architects in London, placed his chair on the conference table and then sat down on it. From the top of this perch he could hammer home his argument to the astonished audience: "Everything is a question of point of view!"

This pathway, installed at Bois des Moutiers in the 1980s, has created a completely new view looking down over the sea of 'Halopeanum' rhododendrons that bloom during May.

"Let me ask you this: Can you dance on your left eye?"
Erik Satie (Relâche, 1924)

Forms, textures, and lighting

Going beyond simple lines, the choice and design of forms can be crucial for the judicious management of the space we are dealing with; this is especially true for smaller gardens. Different leaf shapes can serve to induce our eyes to either pass rapidly over what we see or else to stop and look more closely.

In a situation where architecture is dominant, large leaves are needed—in this case, those of a *Hydrangea sargentiana.* (Bois des Moutiers)

Large in front of small

By placing larger leaves in the foreground and progressively finer ones going back into the distance, we can create the impression of an even larger space. Children, even when they are very young, already convey in their drawings of familiar objects (houses, birds, or trees) that when these are drawn smaller they are supposed to be in the distance.

There is, of course, the special case of shrubs whose small, dark leaves blend together to form a single mass, and which, with their low, compact habit, look rather like rocks. These seem to frame what we see and, therefore, seem to bring the background closer (photo on page 79).

In a setting where architecture is prominent, we should choose plants with large leaves: rounded in front of angular structures, jagged in front of rounded structures (left). The rule of "large in front of small" also makes it easy to understand why evergreen rhododendrons are incompatible with deciduous azaleas. Aside from the fact that their colors often clash, putting the fine foliage of azaleas in front of the heavy foliage of rhododendrons is total nonsense. We need to separate both the colors and the plants themselves, placing them as far apart as possible in the garden.

The large leaves of Indian rhubarb
(*Darmera peltata*) in the middle distance,
in front of the finer foliage of bamboos,
give the impression of a larger space.

The box bushes in the middle distance, clipped into the shape of rocks, catch the eye and push the background farther into the distance. At the same time, the jagged-edged foliage in the foreground contrasts with the round shapes of the clipped box and helps to increase the feeling of space. The diagonal lines converging toward the circular opening created by the branches also guide the eye outward and reinforce the general impression of space in this small garden. (Rowden Garden)

The monkey puzzle tree's prickly and rather forbidding aspect stops visitors in their tracks, leaving them to gradually make out the presence of the subtle and delicate garden beyond. (Jardin de Saboutot, near Doudeville in Normandy.)

Jagged in front of oval and round

Shrubs with foliage that is jagged, lobed, or even armed with spikes have a role to play as menacing-looking guardians. They evoke a feeling of fear and mobilize visitors' attention. Any scene observed from behind such visual barriers takes on the attraction of a secret and forbidden world waiting to be discovered.

Behind this jagged foliage, which can seem a little daunting or off-putting, the rounded or oval shapes of foliage in the background are perceived as more appealing, and their contrast with those in the foreground generates visual space.

Consequently, the coarse leaves of cherry laurel (*Prunus laurocerasus*), aucubas, and even some rhododendrons can be rendered "nicer

Vertical features generally mark a shift toward more or less horizontal expanses. (Château de Val Joannis)

to know" by placing plants in front of them whose jagged-edged leaves are even larger, such as yuccas, New Zealand flax (*Phormium*), or, in more temperate regions, agave. In addition, behind heavy foliage plants it is useful to place plants with finer foliage: bay laurel (*Laurus nobilis*), holm oaks (*Quercus ilex*), various hollies, or dark, matte conifers such as some cypresses.

Vertical in front of horizontal

All trees with a columnar, upright, pyramidal, or erect aspect are naturally suited for foregrounds. Planted in pairs, they create a doorway; in isolation, a signal or landmark. They can serve to frame a courtyard or a clearing, or to punctuate a pathway. They will capture the curiosity of the walker, who will then go on to simultaneously take delight

Two contrasting kinds of landscape: one that actively appeals to the eye (bottom, in Tuscany), and the other that soothes it (top, in Varengeville-sur-Mer, Normandy).

in the other lines of the landscape: the horizon line, furrows in plowed fields, trimmed hedges, well-defined clumps of plants, terraces bordered by balustrades, balconies and bridges with harmonious arches.

There are other vertical signs to be discovered in a landscape: church towers in the countryside, gateways, flagpoles, totem poles, or stone posts at the entrance to a garden. All these tonic accents enhance the beauty of the spaces in the background.

All this helps us to appreciate the charm of the landscapes of Tuscany where tall, slender cypress trees seem to converse with the umbrella pines, and where both sorts of tree are inscribed upon the melodic lines of the hills.

The proportion of vertical and horizontal lines has a direct impact on the character of a landscape: undulating and uneven, or broad, soothing expanses. You can, of course, choose whatever best suits your temperament; but it is certainly very restful, between visiting two gardens, to cross over a vast plain.

Glossy in front of matte, sharply defined in front of blurred, still in front of mobile

The juxtaposition of glossy foliage and matte foliage makes the first seem nearer and the second farther away, which creates additional visual space.

A plant with sharply defined contours positioned in front of a plant with wispy,

Right: Colors ranging from light to dark reinforce the feeling of space. The judicious use of grasses within this small space enlivens the whole composition. (Mark W. Brown)

Below: Perennials with light-colored foliage placed in the foreground give depth to a border.

vaporous foliage (artemisia, tamarisk) creates a visual empty space between the two.

Compact, immobile masses placed in front of mobile and flexible forms open up a field of vision that will encourage daydreaming.

Light in front of dark

In the same vein, light-toned leaves should be placed in front of darker-looking plants. To clearly see differences in the value (that is, luminosity) of each color in a garden, it is a good idea to take pictures in black and white. Colors of the same value have no effect on our perception of their respective distance, whereas very light-colored spots in the foreground immediately give the illusion of depth to a flower bed.

Left: Variegated hollies are an unparalleled resource for bringing light into shady corners. (*Ilex* 'Belgicum Aureum')

Below: *Miscanthus sinensis* 'Variegata'

Variegated plants and colored edges

A significant addition to a garden's character involves making use of plants that are variegated or that have colored edges: silver, gold, or even pink.

This horticultural feature irresistibly attracts visitors' attention because it emphasizes the character of a plant's foliage by highlighting the outline of each leaf, whatever size it may be. One may conjure up evocative memories of silver holly in the distance or of a tulip tree with golden-edged leaves in full evening light.

An excess of variegated plants should be avoided, however: one thinks of the misuse ad nauseam of a poplar with yellow-marked leaves, which was evident almost everywhere in southern Ireland in the 1990s.

Left: Not everyone has enough room to put blue cedars at the bottom of their garden. Fortunately, many plants that take up less space can produce the same effect.

Below: In a walled garden, wisteria is nicer than Virginia creeper as a way of covering up a wall. (Les Colombages, in Varengeville-sur-Mer)

The universal value of backgrounds

In an orchestra, the strings are traditionally placed in front of the wind instruments. In French cuisine, stocks (*fonds de cuisine*) are the secret of great sauces. The art of entertaining involves the choice of good basic company so as to better set off distinguished guests. It is the same for gardens: backgrounds must be planned out very carefully. They should be neither uniform nor all of the same hue.

For backgrounds, never use foliage with large leaves, like the classic Virginia creeper growing on a wall. It draws attention to itself, and in doing so merely reinforces the effect of a barrier. Instead, use much finer leaves with colors in the blue-green range, and evergreen if possible. One thinks immediately of the wide choice offered by different kinds of ivy (whether or not associated with small-leaved vines that change color in autumn), by holly, and especially by conifers—provided that they never occur in continuous hedges (*Leylandii*), which is like locking oneself up in jail.

Finally, remember that if you enjoy the color of evergreens during winter, both spring and autumn will be enlivened by their contrast with the often-colorful foliage of deciduous shrubs.

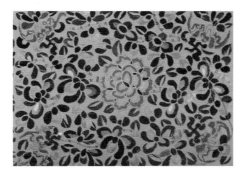

The Shakespeare Garden once designed by Mark W. Brown in Varengeville-sur-Mer was the very model of a composition full of subtlety and nuance.

Nuance rather than contrast

The more nuances there are in shapes, textures, and (luminosity), the greater the feeling of space will be. Conversely, contrasts that are too strong are likely to reduce observation time and thus make large things appear to be smaller than they really are.

Some Chinese embroidery plays on nuances so as to prevent the observer from discovering the whole subject in just one look. If you take time to absorb the myriad details, you will eventually discover a multitude of hidden birds, whereas at first glance only the dots of their eyes stand out. The embroidered picture starts out as a flat image but slowly becomes a vast world to explore.

This attention to nuance is the golden rule for advising all lovers of gardens, because it is within these tiny deviations that dreams are born. The finer the nuances, the more poetic are our thoughts. "*Nuance, seul fiancé*" ("Nuance, our only engagement"), as Verlaine put it.

This rule applies not only for choosing plants to compose the backgrounds of gardens, but also for planning flower beds when they are designed like embroidery. The arts of tapestry and of flower arranging are the best schools for refining the way you look at things.

Another view in a different range of colors by the same designer.

Softness rather than harshness

We have often seen meticulously cared-for gardens located in affluent neighborhoods of large cities. A search for easy maintenance and the urge toward social conformity result in an appearance that is so clean, so orderly, that it is commonplace and totally devoid of originality. The contours and shapes are too sharp and produce an impression of hardness that is the result of too much contrast.

We argue for more gentleness, softer lines, more poetry, more expansiveness, and more misty and undefined effects. Modern life makes quite enough demands on our poor, tired eyes.

They will find rest by contemplating compositions that are easy to read, without harshness, with delicate tones, like petit point embroidery. All this would surely improve the quality of human relations and liberate our space. We should "try a little tenderness" in our gardens!

Left: The exotic water garden by Jean Lebret (Clos du Coudray). Many new exotic plants can be used today.

Above: The feathery effect of *Miscanthus* at Jardin Plume.

New gardens, new plants

As the famous Brazilian landscape architect and botanist Roberto Burle Marx said, you can only create "new gardens" with new plants. The incredible selection of new plants available to everyone these days gives even inexperienced gardeners the option of doing innovative work, even and especially if it is based on successful experiments they see around them.

In this respect, the field of possibilities is immense.

Right: Two plants from Japan, *Aralia elata* and *Hydrangea paniculata* (here the variety 'Floribunda').

Below: These two new plants, introduced in the 1980s, make a strong impression: *Eleagnus* 'Quick Silver' and *Ceanothus* 'Italian Blue'. (Bois des Moutiers)

Family resemblance

Every gardener who knows a little bit about plants will have noticed that plants originating from the same country or the same habitat have an air of complicity: they go well together. From their apparent contentment, we ourselves derive a sense of calm.

We cannot recommend strongly enough grouping Japanese plants together (photo above); the same goes for Chinese or Chilean plants and, of course, for all plants belonging to the same habitat. This, incidentally, is the idea behind some modern public gardens.

The most recent idea is to collect plants that are close together in the phylogenetic tree determined by DNA analysis. In this way, ancient and unsophisticated plants dating from the time of the dinosaurs could be planted together—or then again, much more recent plants whose family relationship may be surprising, such as that between *Hydrangea* and *Cornus*.

Pergolas, porticos, frames, arbors, bowers

If we assume that any built element has to fit into a framework designed to enlarge space in the garden, there are many options for new gardeners.

By installing pergolas, porticos, and different kinds of metal frames, we can open up all sorts of possibilities for growing different climbing plants, such as wisteria, roses, and clematis.

Arbors and bowers (hornbeam being a classic choice, but not the only one) can act as shady passageways that rest our eyes and mind while we walk from one garden area to another.

Shapes and perspective

If care has been taken within a given space to observe the rules of perspective so as to encourage the eye to look outward toward the distance, then just one object (bench, obelisk, rock) that is out of proportion with the rest, that is not in the same register as the general plan, will destroy the magic of illusion for which such efforts have been made.

Therefore, flower beds designed in the shape of islands should be treated appropriately, in accordance with the laws of perspective. A flower bed in the rough shape of a butterfly, for example, should be tilted to a sufficient angle and the outline distorted so that it enters visually into the general scheme. This applies to flower beds of any shape (pitchers, pears, and even the perennial beans). Generally, before permanently establishing a new bed, it is better to experiment with a model to get an idea of the final effect. The visual distortions induced by the physical nature of a particular place are such that a mere two-dimensional plan is never adequate.

Sculptures

There are many successful examples of the use of sculpture in gardens, but plenty of far less fortunate experiments also exist. Sculptures have such possibilities as visual attention-getters that we really cannot consider doing without this form of art. It is, however, once again advisable to experiment with models before definitively installing sculptures, especially very heavy works of art that are difficult or impossible to move again once they have been put in place.

Putting a romantic statue in place requires great delicacy. (Right, Jardin d'Angélique, and below, Denmans, England, designed by John Brookes)

Pyramids and other architectural structures

The pyramid is particularly interesting. It is, like the obelisk, a symbol of fire from above, capable of breaking the monotony of a scene by bringing strong punctuation to it. It may be three- or four-sided, conical, mounted on a base or directly on the ground, solid or hollow, with or without doors. It could be used as an effective replacement for the unsightly shacks that normally serve as tool sheds. Prince Hermann von Pückler-Muskau chose the pyramid form for his mausoleum at Branitz. It is used as a symbolic element in the Désert de Retz, was intentionally introduced by Carmontelle in the Parc Monceau (left), and can be found in other parks for the symbolically minded.

Architectural features in general are, like sculptures, a matter of personal taste. Rather than making them serve as a strong contrast with the general harmony by using clashing colors or shapes, it is usually better to fit them into a coherent whole, whatever its inspiration: natural, modern, or exotic.

Attempts to imitate too many different styles in one place will usually only create a sense of incongruity or pointlessness, inevitably leading to an end result that is distressingly ugly. It is, however, possible for true artists to succeed in marrying styles into a coherent whole because they are able to choose a main theme that gives unity to their work.

Sparing use of topiary

Artificial shapes in clipped box or yew, or even ivy growing on a fence, are evident more and more often in gardens. Like statues, these have a clear role as visual attention-getters. More or less decorative, evocative, or even grotesque, they can serve as a way of artificially punctuating space. These curious forms are most often of dark appearance and act as "seamarks," useful aids to navigation in our voyage through the garden.

However, overuse of topiary shrubs should be avoided—not only for visual reasons, but also because maintaining them can quickly take far too much of the owner's time.

Left: Delirium at Disneyland. What's the betting that they've also got square roots!

Opposite: The gardener's well-ordered handiwork suddenly appears in this gap in an otherwise wild-looking copse. (Jardin d Albarède, Dordogne, designed by S. Lapouge)

For some time now, box has gotten back its credentials. There is a choice of many different varieties suitable for original topiary. (Argences Manor, Cotentin, Normandy)

Balls of box, balls of mistletoe

If balls of box seem to be a "must" in contemporary gardens, as trimmed lime hedges were in their time, a decorative element that has been little used and yet looks very pleasing is that of balls of mistletoe in trees. Easy to put in place, the ancient and legendary mistletoe plant is also an indispensable part of traditional Christmas decorations.

Accidents of nature and other curiosities

Trying too hard to copy nature is the sign of a poor gardener. Anyone who has recently acquired a garden and has the good fortune to discover natural accidents and other monsters of nature—twisted branches, gnarled trunks, stones with multiple strata, picturesque forms of all kinds—should take particular care to keep and make use of them.

An artist who takes possession of a small abandoned wood will delight in the natural forms found within it and will use them wisely so as to emphasize them, making sure their beauty remains intact.

Imported objects are harder to deal with. The transportation and installation

of unusual-looking rocks is an art that requires long practice and that cannot just be learned from a book. (But, regarding this, see the book *Jardin au Naturel* by Michel Racine, Acte Sud, 2001.)

In search of curious and unexpected effects, many people use driftwood, pebbles sculpted by the sea, or pieces of broken glass worn into pebbles—treasures collected by beachcombers to be used in rockeries, mosaics, or mobiles.

Above: Curious and amusing objects provide endless sources of surprise and can be used unsparingly. (Garden of La Blanche Maison, Urville-Nacqueville)

Right: Example of a creation based on glass pebbles (designed by Mark W. Brown).

This rusty old bike, straight out of a bygone age, awakens nostalgia for the good old days. (Garden of La Maison Baudy, Giverny, Normandy)

Surprise effects, quirks, amazing or funny things

Unexpected, absurd, and impossible shapes are a good way to provoke surprise, astonishment and laughter. For example, composite creatures have always disturbed the imagination: fauns, centaurs, and mermaids must all have been surprising when they were invented. Today the industry of the image never stops creating all kinds of more or less terrifying or amusing monsters, many of which are downright ugly. There is room for humor in a garden: the absurd repetition of everyday objects, putting conventional forms to unconventional uses, and so on. Some iconoclastic spirits even make a specialty of it; the surrealists made it their watchword.

Better than a picture, this scene combines the effects of contrast, nuances, textures, and animation. (Les Jardins d Ombre et Lumière, created for a stand at Courson)

Bandwagon effect and boredom

Crazes for a particular type of garden emerge in every period: sad gardens of clipped box and evergreens in Holland, light gardens of grasses, mineral gardens (using rock, concrete, or pavement) in towns, and so on. The repetition of gardens that follow a trend in this way fairly soon provokes a sense of déjà vu and ennui.

Accumulation of special effects

In this overview of ways and means to expand our environment, it is important to note that their effects may be combined, which reinforces their power. Thus a beam of light passing through a curtain of mist will be more remarkable if it acquires movement. If, in addition, color is added to these luminous rays, the effect will be even more striking.

This accumulation of special effects can multiply the possibilities for unprecedented creative effects that will challenge understanding.

Colors

"I've seen ones that were yellow, green, red, purple and blue. I've seen ones that were gaping toward heaven, Flowers open like eyes."
Maurice Carême (*Au clair de la lune*, 1977)

"Color is the most potent weapon in a gardener's armory."
Andrew Lawson (*The Gardener's Book of Color*, 1996)

Surprising as it may seem, the judicious use of color can completely transform our perception of space to make it appear larger than life. We have seen in the previous chapter how it is possible to play on degrees of lighting to give an artificial sense of depth to a landscape scene. That leaves two more elements of color to analyze: hue and saturation.

Ancillary effects of color

The complex chemistry of vegetable, animal, or mineral pigments is at the origin of an amazing diversity of colors, semi-tones, and quarter-tones, which are evident, for example, in the thousands of different shades found in an Aubusson tapestry. Today digital imaging technology has gone well past the development stage and has reached a point that staggers our comprehension. Frequency analysis, made possible by new technologies, provides additional knowledge about the nature of a particular color. It has thus been determined that gemstones have very specific frequencies, which, it is said, could make them useful for therapeutic purposes.

Chromotherapy is now accepted as an alternative treatment for depressive illness. We are, in fact, very sensitive to the colors of our environment—to the point that exposure to violent or garish colors can actually lead to brutal behavior. This is also true for some music.

Conversely, a choice of pure and refined colors in our gardens will cause elation and lead us to see our environment in a different light.

Opposite: Blue cedars form an ideal background to showcase the colors of Japanese maples. (Bois des Moutiers)

Below: Yellow-green foliage placed in front of blue-green foliage contributes to an increased feeling of depth.

Color ranges in nature

The world of plants comprises two major color groups: the yellow range and the blue range. We thus have reds in the yellow range giving orange, and reds in the blue range giving purple, and, similarly, yellow greens and blue greens. A little practice makes it easy to recognize the distinction between the yellow range and blue range when we look around.

Yellow range in front of blue range

A plant from the yellow range should always be placed in front of a plant from the blue range.

This is the golden rule for obtaining a sense of depth. It connects with the art of painting, particularly Italian Renaissance landscape painting. Bluish, misty backgrounds (the *sfumato* method) were used to highlight characters dressed in red and gold in the foreground.

Above: Successful handling of crimson, set off by grays, pinks, and pale blue. (Stourton House)

Opposite: This combination of warm and cold colors creates space where almost none exists. The red climbing plant is the flame flower, *Tropaeolum speciosum*. (Stourton House)

Cold colors in front of warm colors

Each color in the yellow or blue range gradually shifts from cold to warmer. With the yellow range of colors, you start with a very pale, icy yellow and then move toward increasingly rich yellows going toward orange, then scarlet, and finally crimson and then brownish-black. The blue range is more subtle, beginning with a cold, sad blue-gray and finishing with royal blue, purple, and deep black.

Within both ranges, it is essential to observe the order going from the coldest to the warmest in order to obtain a feeling of space.

The different shades of blue in the foreground have a soothing effect and lead our rested eyes toward the unobtrusive opening in the shadows of the background. (Parham House Gardens)

Blue: A very special color

Blue reduces the effect of glare from light that is too strong. Indeed, although our eyes are able to see in conditions ranging from a very weak half-light (10–20 lux) to full sunlight (100,000 lux), it takes time for them to adjust to change. This is why when you leave a dark cellar you are dazzled by the light of day, and when you go inside again it takes some time for your eyes to be able to distinguish anything at all. Blue light can reduce this adaptation time significantly. There was a time when cars had a blue bulb attached to the corner of the windshield to prevent drivers from being dazzled by the headlights of oncoming cars. This is also why very lightly colored flowers, such as very pale pink, are perceived as white in France south of the

Above: The blue color placed next to these peonies prevents dazzling and allows us to enjoy every nuance of their delicate flowers.

Below: The blue color in the foreground allows our eyes to distinguish the details of the background without fatigue. (Rainbow kitchen garden, Château de Bosmelet, Normandy)

Loire but as delicately colored in the north; in the northern regions the bluish color of the shadows rests our eyes, enabling them to distinguish all the nuances. The same applies to the eyes' ability to distinguish among white flowers of different shades.

Another example of this phenomenon: in a brand new office facility, lighting had been planned with a power of 600 lux. The secretaries were dazzled by the glare reflected from their typewriter keys. They quickly showed signs of conjunctivitis and all started wearing dark glasses. The lamp bulbs were replaced with other slightly bluish ones of the same power, and the problem was instantly resolved.

The color blue can also expand our visual angle. This intangible angle, at the foundation of all architectural measurements, is also different depending on whether the site is in full sun or shade. What are the consequences for the organization of the garden? If blue in the distance (real or artificial) increases the feeling of space, this color also helps us to see farther and more clearly—in exactly the same way we avoid being dazzled by lowering the sun visor of our car or by shading our eyes with our hand. There is an immediate physical sensation of rest for the eyes, the same as what we feel when going into the shade after spending time in bright sunlight.

Similarly, when blue is placed in the foreground in front of a panoramic landscape, the eye is able to take in a wider angle and we are thus able to enjoy it more completely.

Finally, when blue is placed close to colors that are too loud, it can mitigate the violence of contrasts and make us better able to distinguish nuances.

Perception of the color red according to gender

It seems that men and women perceive the color red differently because it is associated with the concept of danger. Women, fierce guardians of life, seem to detect it more quickly, even at a distance: red traffic lights or warning signals, for example. Men are apparently slower to realize that the color is there: it has to be placed closer to them. We can imagine some fine domestic scenes when it comes to choosing where to plant that red rhododendron!

The case of the color purple

Many of us have been tempted at some time to buy a plant with purple foliage: a hazel, a copper beech, a smoke bush (*Cotinus* 'Royal Purple'), or an eastern redbud (*Cercis canadensis* 'Forest Pansy'). This color, sought after by growers, can sometimes unexpectedly occur in nature.

The difficult part comes next, however, because we have to find a suitable location for the plant in the garden. A range of monochrome purple combines perfectly with the pink of apple blossom, for example, or with mauves, violets, and blue-greens, but it clashes with the yellow-green of lawns and meadows.

Purple appears warmer when juxtaposed with orange (photo opposite). Purple foliage should be placed at the bottom of the garden, separated from grassland by buffers of shrubs, which may be gray (*Eleagnus* 'Quick Silver'), pink, or purple (peonies, lilacs, roses, wisteria, etc.), or else backed up against dark green (boxwood, *Phillyrea*, *Viburnum tinus*, or some of the more bluish-green yews).

Above: The purplish foliage of this fennel brilliantly highlights the orange of the poppies, whereas lemon yellow would have been garish.

Opposite: A vivid demonstration of the effect of chromatic contrast: a stained glass effect for the two colors in the foreground (see also photo, page 109, right), and an effect of distance for the two colors of the background. The light color in the middle is common to both foreground and background.

Delicate or saturated colors

Horticulturists often deliberately try to obtain bright, garish colors. Garden center chains prefer to stock plants that stimulate impulse purchases all by themselves. So we are invaded by flashy, "look at me" plants, and all this puts a severe strain on our sensibility. Should we just blame the professionals? No, because we also have to take into account the obvious need of our contemporaries for thrills. The Swiss psychiatrist Carl Jung gave a convincing explanation: we spend our time occupied with mainly intellectual activities; working in offices, we place far fewer demands on our sensory functions, which therefore require much stronger stimuli to awaken them.

Just like children coming out of school, most of our contemporaries feel an irre-

Above: This composition, all in different shades of yellow, was created by the remarkable colorist Mark W. Brown. (*Paeonia* 'Moonlight', *Rosa pimpinifolia* 'Old Double Yellow Scotch')

Right: Spotted rhododendrons are the epitome of flowers with unsaturated colors. (Bois des Moutiers)

pressible desire for thrills. This explains the popularity of violent movies, abuse of all kinds, and the need for striking and saturated colors.

The tragedy is that when exposed to all this, our senses become dulled and require more and more stimulation to produce the same effect. So we find ourselves flooded out with acres and acres of brightly colored tulips and garish azaleas with names like 'Satan' and 'Lucifer' (sic!).

In this way, our capacity for fine and sensitive feelings shrinks away to nothing; and also, with it, our potential for feeling pleasure.

Let us therefore give more priority to colors in half or quarter tones. Plants with these colors are unfortunately not very widespread on the market (there is a similar poverty of choice in the range of colors available for embroidery and knitting). Yet such delicately colored plants can refine our senses and thus extend our range of sensations. Perhaps we should seek to emulate the Persian poet who was content to contemplate a single rose in a vase, from the first bud to the tragic fall of the last petal. In our French gardens, we are now often limited to "fast food"—a long way from the wealth of traditional French gastronomy. Fortunately, the trend is reversing and many are now looking for flowers with delicate colors. At "Garden Days" at Courson (near Paris) and elsewhere, artist gardeners can at last find happiness.

Among the flowers that present different colors and different degrees of saturation, we may note shrub or herbaceous peonies, Japanese irises (*Iris ensata*), and rhododendrons with spotted flower heads (with something that looks like a bumblebee at the heart of each flower).

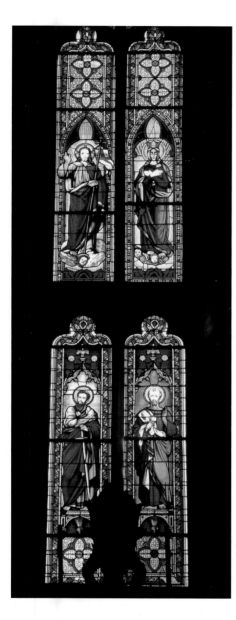

Stained glass effects can be obtained by placing golden yellow behind red, which has the effect of flattening the perspective. The effect of stained glass is even more striking when medieval colors are used. (*Acer* 'Benikagami' and faded astilbes, Bois des Moutiers)

Medieval Colors

For those who are not attracted by pastel colors, there is a range of colors that is both strong and gentle. These are medieval colors, inspired by gemstones.

Looking for stained glass colors in plants, we can create some really sublime scenes: the deep blue of certain hydrangeas, the velvety red of our grandmothers' roses, the clean white of lilies, combined with the golden yellow of brocades and the greens and browns of old Italian velvet. It is in cathedrals that we can discover the cosmic scale of certain compositions and the interplay of colors among them. The red of the stained glass windows in Chartres cathedral projects its complementary green color onto the gold of the candle flames, which seems cooler and purer when compared with the glowing red of the stained glass. It is indeed touching to see how these masterpieces, more than eight centuries old, can still spontaneously produce in us such feelings of peace and open-mindedness.

Projection of the complementary color

This is not the place to explain and develop the modern theory of color. Excellent books are available specifically to illuminate those who wish to understand how it operates. One well-known phenomenon, however, deserves to be mentioned: we project onto surrounding colors the color that is complementary to the one we are observing. So blues seem bluer if we first stare at orange, yellow seems more yellow if we saturate ourselves with purple. Moreover, so-called "illusory" colors result from the interaction of different adjoining colors. But knowledge of these phenomena has not seen much use yet in floral arrangements.

Subjective colors: Young-Helmholtz theory, color blindness

A light surface is seen as red when situated behind a dark element, but it is seen as blue when located in front of a dark background. The interplay of black and white masses therefore induces subjective colors, which we should take into account when composing garden scenes. This may be an advantage where blue sublimates a gray that would otherwise be dull, but it can be a drawback where red turns what you hoped was bright green into brown.

The stars of the golden *Euryops* appear more yellow as we project the complementary color of the blue *Agastache* onto them (top). The same phenomenon (bottom) with the orange *Cosmos sulphureus* in front of the smoke bush *Cotinus coggygria* 'Royal Purple'.

A garden made entirely of exotic foliage can provoke a feeling of disorientation simply through the shapes of the leaves. (*Phormium* and Eucalyptus in the garden of the Château de Vauville in Normandy)

The difficulty of seeing certain colors could lead some people to create gardens made primarily of textures and shapes, playing on values. But an inability to see the disharmony between certain colors—or, in contrast, their sublime combination—is also a matter of culture in which learning plays an important role. By dint of exposure to colors that are uninteresting or worse, the public has acquired questionable primary tastes. One can hope, however, that a natural desire to always taste the very best will lead to progress in the art of floral composition.

The handling of whites requires a delicate touch. (Valerian *Centranthus ruber* 'Albus' and 'Iceberg' rose)

The use of white, black, and gray: non-colors

Contrary to popular belief, white does not attract the eye but repels it. The eye looks for rest and, in doing so, naturally inclines toward black. This does not mean that white is not noticeable. It actually tends to monopolize our vision, so that white dominates what we see. This is particularly true in moonlight. Dark corners become like doors opening to a mysterious other world. Shiny leaves become lanterns, and statues look like ghosts.

Those who seek to create white gardens (gray and white, or green and white, depending on the degree of sunlight) are often unfairly accused of snobbery on the grounds that some very well-known gardens have launched a fashion for them. White, like green, is difficult to use in painting. Some whites tinged with yellow look dirty when put next to pure, brilliant white; this is not the case for white tinged with pink. The handling of white requires extreme delicacy!

Paradoxically, monochrome gardens offer many opportunities to bring together

A Persian garden, where the choice of strictly authentic plants requires scholarly research from its creator. (Damask rose *Rosa* 'Omar Khayyam', stock *Matthiola incana*, and *Iris florentina*)

and showcase the myriad nuances that it is possible to obtain with just one color. *The Gardener's Book of Color* by Andrew Lawson (Readers Digest, 1996) is a bible in this regard.

In defense of the color black, we can say that like gray, this non-color with its many nuances is able to highlight all other colors and thus bring thickness and depth to any color composition. But an excess of black (black tulips, purple sage, etc.) has an air of mourning, even though sad souls may find that this harmonizes with their mood.

The use of non-colors (white, black, and gray) to distinguish the lines of garden structures or furniture does not just correspond with passing fads. The use of these non-colors is justified by the very fact that they stand out against an otherwise colorful ensemble.

Above: The flower meadow is a gift from nature to any garden in the first stage of its development. (Longueil, Normandy)

Opposite: Effects of simultaneous lengthening and narrowing of space, in a composition demonstrating constant movement. (Mark W. Brown).

False colors

If color and brightness are perceived by different types of neurons within the retina, then one can imagine that composite colors, whose multiple wavelengths travel to different visual circuits, produce visual confusion, difficult for the brain to identify. Once again, this would produce a certain fuzziness that would have the effect of abnormally retaining the viewer's attention. But is this not exactly what some are looking for in a plant? The problem with these false colors is that it is very difficult to combine them with other, more defined colors; if we find harmony with one of the colors in such an "alloy," the other color will often be discordant.

Flower beds and flower meadows

A free introductory gift for the novice gardener, flowery meadows demand poor, rather than rich, soil. Simple harrowing followed by timely sowing is enough to adorn a hitherto untouched space with multiple colors. Later the beginner can invest in the appropriate amendments to create real flower beds: places for monochrome or multicolored creations in which the field of possibilities is endless.

Opposite effects and simultaneous effects

It is easy for anyone to observe how the optical effects described in this book can serve to make any part of the garden seem more distant, but we must not forget that these effects work in both directions. So if we place a warm color is placed in front of a cool color, for example, we can reduce rather than increase the feeling of distance.

This is particularly useful for the window dresser's art. Items in the shop window must catch the eye to attract the potential buyer. It is also true for glass artists. What could

be called the stained glass window effect is due to the fact that red, for instance, placed behind a web of blue, will seem to come forward through the cracks, accentuating the richness and beauty of the color.

If these effects work both ways, then we can consider using them simultaneously and thereby create a sensation of movement. For example, this illusion could be put into practice by visual juxtaposition in a flower bed, where a few spots of white would occur in the foreground, followed by mauve, followed by purple (lengthening effect), then immediately afterwards followed by light

gray (stained glass effect). The light-colored touches of the background will literally cross over the purple screen to harmonize with the white spots of the foreground. One can imagine an almost infinite number of such compositions. Here the garden artist's composition process is similar to that employed by impressionist and pointillist painters who used these principles to bring light into their works, which often seem to spring out from their canvases. In small spaces, it can be used to sublimate warm colors by propelling them through darker ones placed in the foreground (photo overleaf).

Mixing textures, shapes, and colors

The same goes for textures as for lighting, as both of them reflect more or less light. To become more conscious of this, an amusing exercise is to go to your local greengrocer, buy different varieties of vegetables, and then try to arrange them in a certain order: from lighter to darker; from duller to glossier; from the coolest to the warmest tones; within the yellow or blue color range or in the order of the colors of the rainbow; from round shapes to elongated ones. Then you can ask different questions: why put the cauliflower in the foreground, for example?

Whether in the family or at school, this game will make anyone and everyone more aware of the rich palette of colors, shapes, and textures that nature gives us.

In the garden, successful examples of mixing flowers and fruit together have brought a real originality to what would otherwise be more conventional compositions: purplish apples combined with white tobacco flowers, and so on.

Movements, colors, and illusions

Streams have been discovered in Cambodia where the beds are paved with mosaics representing deities, who are gently caressed by the moving water so as to yield up all sorts of blessings and benefits. The paving is terra-cotta, whose glowing reddish tones can be glimpsed through the bubbling ripples and eddies.

On these running or still waters, one can sometimes observe floating elements such as maple leaves in autumn or deliberately scattered flower petals.

They create the illusion that they are floating in air rather than water. This effect also can sometimes be seen with water lilies.

Curious effects are produced when we look through windows of blown glass. If we move slightly from right to left, parallel to the window, we will see a landscape that is veiled and in motion.

Looking out over a garden, installations can be put in place made of vertical panes of glass over which a uniform curtain of water runs; these provide a blurred but esthetic vision of the garden's myriad colors. Depending on the angle of exterior lighting, the eye will also see partially diffracted flashes of light in addition to the general multicolored effect.

To close off a garden without hiding the view from outside, one can use extremely fine wire mesh; its transparency gives an uninterrupted, sometimes shimmering, view of the garden scene behind it.

Opposite: Mixture of shapes and colors producing a stained glass effect. The warm colors of the castor oil plant placed in front of the white flowers of *Nicotiana* literally gush out of the composition. (Longueil, Normandy)

Right: A streambed paved with pebbles. This could take the form of a mosaic or images of deities, as found in Cambodia. These decorative or sacred elements highlight the movement of the water, which can sometimes be designed as a sort of permanent prayer. (Jardin d'Angélique)

Below: Votive tree by Emma Schercliff, Bois des Moutiers, 2002. Such installations by contemporary artists in classical gardens can enliven parts of the gardens that seem dull out of season.

Stained glass color projections

We admire the splashes of color projected onto the pillars of a church by stained glass windows. Effects like these have not yet fully found their rightful place in our interiors. Yet neighborhood legislation is generally more tolerant, so as to allow translucent walls when opening windows is forbidden by law.

Coats of arms, flags, and banners

Pieces of colored cloth have served throughout history to distinguish one clan from another, to indicate which side someone is on, or to attract the attention of the spirits of place. Every period and every country has its flags. Mounted on poles, they are vertical bridges to put humans in touch with the elements and the forces of heaven. On calm days they indicate peaceful weather. In high winds they keep us alert. Like the sails of a boat constantly surveyed by the helmsman, the movement of flags inevitably captures our attention.

Timothy Hennessy's large banners enlivened the upper part of the Parc des Moutiers for a whole summer. However, it was important to make sure they were brought in before storms started.

During the summer of 2002 in the same park, a votive tree was chosen on whose branches visitors could tie a ribbon and their wish. Similar wishes soon festooned other trees nearby, too.

If we imagine these banners made out of reflective material, they would reflect the beauty of the sky or of neighboring trees.

Colors and reflections

During the same summer at the Parc des Moutiers, a contemporary art installation played on the principles of color and reflection.

Basing her creation on a pink rhododendron mirrored in a pond, the artist (Sari Myöhännen) inserted rods through the surface of the water, each one topped with a cube of the same color. By extrapolating from this garden scene, she managed to create a true work of art (see opposite).

Coastal gardens often enjoy effects of morning mist that are sometimes crossed by almost miraculous rays of sunlight like the beams of a spotlight.

ways. But we should not forget that nature sometimes comes up with much better effects than we could produce ourselves (photos this page and opposite).

For very special occasions (parties, weddings, etc.), we can devise rains of confetti and other light objects. In autumn, falling leaves make us glad or sad.

We should also remember the beautiful carpets of flower petals laid out in convents or in public streets to brighten religious festivals: a tradition that still exists in some countries (Infiorata in Italy, for example). These intricate compositions have a certain ritualistic aspect that is close to Asian traditions.

Among well-identified flying objects, it remains to discuss the winged kind: free flights of doves or pigeons, or other birds with colorful and varied plumage that can harmonize with plants close to their natural habitat, as in traditional Chinese paintings and tapestries.

Butterflies are attracted to fragrant shrubs such as buddleia. If you want to encourage them, you should allow some caterpillars to survive; or you can consider breeding them, so as to enjoy the spectacle of these tenuous, multicolored creatures dancing in the light. Collecting melliferous plants in the garden attracts bees and other pollen-gathering insects that will fill the air with their busy hum; this is particularly satisfying for people who are aural rather than visual.

The surface of ponds attracts dragonflies and other insects that feed on mosquito larvae. But the real surprise comes from multicolored koï carp, whose sudden appearance

Smoke, feathers, scales
Different opportunities are available for changing the look of a garden by using colored light or even curtains of smoke, wisps of steam, or will-o'-the-wisps that seem to emanate from swamps. Devices are available today that deliver such vapors, colored or not, that can be illuminated in a thousand

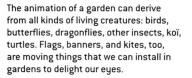

The animation of a garden can derive from all kinds of living creatures: birds, butterflies, dragonflies, other insects, koï, turtles. Flags, banners, and kites, too, are moving things that we can install in gardens to delight our eyes.

Opposite, bottom: The Rainbow vegetable garden at Bosmelet is an amazing achievement, to be enjoyed and wondered at from summer to late autumn.

will astonish people looking into the water. The design of the pond can be important: one can accentuate the effect of surprise if the pond has overhanging edges.

Kites, soap bubbles, rainbows

For the joy of children and the admiration of all, entertaining special effects can be installed in the garden using limited, inexpensive resources.

If the weather is right, fixing a colorful kite at the end of a cable creates a true visual event in which we can all express our creativity.

Soap bubbles created by a blast of air blown through soapy water are one of the happy "happenings" that are easy to put into practice. These bubbles, lightly col-

ored by the products they are made of, are also naturally tinged with the colors of the rainbow.

We will end this chapter on color where it could have begun. The theme of the rainbow has been little used, with the exception of the Rainbow vegetable garden at the Château de Bosmelet (below). By using a sprinkler system to create a mist, suitably lit by lateral sunlight, we could make this sublime optical phenomenon appear on demand in the garden.

If such an effect were associated with a flight of doves, blind indeed would be those who did not understand the message!

The other senses in action

It may seem surprising to find reflections on sounds and smells in a book on vision. Yet it is a fact that our other senses reinforce the impact of the image and thereby contribute to what we see. It would be impossible today to imagine releasing a film without an appropriate soundtrack. In a garden the sense of smell brings its own sensations, making us use our eyes to find the plant that is the source of an attractive scent. Proprioception, a kind of sixth sense, is also capable of improving the way we see. Even the sense of touch cannot be excluded from the process of vision.

All the senses are interconnected

The connection among the five or six senses was known and discussed even before Marcel Proust used his famous *madeleine* to illustrate the concept of involuntary memory. For all such memories are in some way attached to a long-ago sensory experience. The vision of a place known in childhood, or just part of that place, can bring back all the atmosphere of our past life.

The latest findings on neuronal function confirm, and indeed go beyond, what was until recently still in the domain of observation. A neuron can have up to 10,000 connections with other neurons to form an infinite number of different circuits. And all this is not static; on the contrary, it is being built up continuously. Even more remarkable: our behavior when using one sense—touch, for example—can be directly influenced by another mental activity, like song or speech. Try getting a large, well-grown plant into the trunk of your car without breaking a single one of its branches. The only way you can possibly do it is by speaking to it gently! This explains the benefit of working to the sound of music or in scented air.

Pleasant noise and noise pollution

The noise of city traffic is likely to get in the way of the pleasure of visiting a garden. But the pleasant sound of a fountain or a waterfall is capable of masking and blurring the surrounding hubbub (as in the Japanese Garden at the Albert Kahn Gardens in Boulogne-Billancourt near Paris).

Music can help us to see better and more intensely. Hearing opens the view. For birds, the amorous song of the male has always been a way to improve the chosen one's "view" of him. The virtuosity of a bird's trills is exquisite music for us, too, and a powerful way to awaken our own view of the world, freeing us from all sorts of concerns and thereby enabling us to take in the full measure of the beauty around us. Harmonious sounds help us to see more intensely.

Birdsong, aviaries, exotic recordings

From a single nightingale in a cage to large aviaries in zoos, there is an infinite variety of birdsong. Caged birds are very popular in China; their owners bring them into public parks to compare their merits.

Recordings of the cries of gulls on the coast or of exotic birds calls are capable of transporting us to other places and transforming our world in no time at all.

Voices of trees

Trees emit different sounds when the wind blows through them. Following the example of primitive burial grounds where the voices of the dead could be heard in the wind in the trees, we should be conscious of this world of sound, using it to compose our own "sonatas."

Musical and pictorial tones

There is a striking correspondence between musical tone and color tone. Some painters and musicians can talk forever about it, finding connections between certain colors and different musical keys. We can imagine visiting a garden where the sounds of music are associated with different color schemes.

Sounds and movements

It would be difficult to "pass over in silence" the wonderfully refreshing gurgle of small streams or the crystal tones of a little waterfall. The sudden rain in some Japanese gardens can immediately transform nature, silent and motionless a moment ago, into a real orchestra of fluid and varied sounds coming from all sides. Who would not welcome the rain in such circumstances?

Movement produced by the wind is something else we can count on to open up space. The eye is naturally attracted to anything that moves: "quaking aspen" poplars that suddenly turn to shimmering silver with the sound of a waterfall, or a simple breeze rustling through bamboo. Be on the lookout for anything that moves! From grasses to great trees, all plants have their own song, especially when the wind blows through them.

Opposite: Like thirsty explorers attracted by the distant babbling of a brook, visitors cannot fail to direct their steps toward the source of this promising sound. (Le Clos de Coudray)

At the entrance to a lawn, a carpet of Roman chamomile (*Chamaemelum nobile* 'Treneague') acts as a scented foot bath, especially when we walk barefoot through it.

Delicious or pungent scents

The sense of smell deserves a detailed study all to itself. Of all the senses, this one is the most directly connected to the brain, as if nature had deliberately endowed us with the most effective possible instrument of perception, to warn us in real time of an event (the smell of fire or the proximity of a living being, whether threatening or benevolent) or of a particular plant (whether useful or dangerous). Some odors are indeed particularly useful, being associated with food (depending on the degree of cooking), cleanliness (or not), health (medicinal plants), desire (pheromones), and the sacred (incense).

Smells arouse our attention and incite us to look for their source (whether pleasant or otherwise). This behavior has very real implications for our perception of space. A fragrance reaches us and permeates the entire space.

Conversely, the sight of a plant known for its scent can conjure up the memory of its perfume. Thus seeing a picture of mimosa, lily of the valley, violets, or roses can trigger a sensation of the corresponding scent. There are those who have been tempted to impose an order on the succession of different scents and flavors in their garden: from sweet to salty and bitter, passing through acid; from light to heavy and heady. In season, magnolias, lilacs, viburnum, daphne, and roses can represent steps along the way during a walk through the garden.

Proprioception and touch

Defined by the dictionary as "the sensitivity of bones, muscles, tendons and joints, providing information on static equilibration and the movement of the body through space," proprioception allows us to feel whether our path is going upward or downward, is straight or curved, sandy or muddy, or if the stairs we are on are difficult or easy to climb (in particular, whether they respect the ideal proportion between height and tread: see Blondel's formula on page 143).

Proprioception associated with the senses of touch and hearing helps us to identify the nature of the ground beneath our feet: sand or gravel, brick paving or stone paving, more or less polished, more or less resonant. If we are aware of this sensitivity, we can introduce into our gardens all kinds of breaks, contrasts, shades, and nuances to trick our senses and thus increase the apparent size of the space we have entered.

Touch and sight: Gardens for the visually impaired

The sense of touch has a key role in shaping the vision of newborn babies. It is touch that enables the baby to distinguish up from down—that is to say, the mirror image of what is actually projected onto the retina.

For the visually impaired, touch is the sense that is most used to replace that of sight. Gardens designed for them consist primarily of plants that are remarkable for their shape, texture, or scent (when rubbing their leaves). It is important to limit the number of such plants, however, because the time needed to appreciate them in this way is much longer than when using sight. The notion of space is, therefore, quite different for the visually impaired.

The senses and movement

All these methods of increasing the space of our gardens are only half useful unless we are encouraged to walk around them in all directions: by the murmur of a waterfall that gets louder as we approach it; by a scent that becomes more insistent as we come closer to its source; by pathways that become softer to walk on as we near a particular destination. The garden designer can make a feature of pathways that lead us, sometimes unwittingly, to unexpected places.

The effect of waterfalls and cataracts

During the first few minutes of Werner Herzog's film *Heart of Glass*, viewers are subjected to the image of a huge waterfall that fills the entire screen.

This provokes a strange feeling, making you feel as though you are floating upward, rising from your seat.

In some public garden squares in the United States, walls of water not only provide a physical sensation of freshness but also give this strange impression of levitation.

The same effect occurs when sitting in a stationary train in a station: when another train seen through the window starts moving, we feel as if we are going backward.

It is possible to harness this illusion to create an impression of movement, but this time of the landscape itself. If we take a boat trip along the canals of the Wörlitzer Park in Germany or through the Marais Poitevin marshes in France, the silent progress of the boat through the water can make us believe that it is the landscape, not our boat, that is moving.

If we lack space in the garden to install a Niagara Falls, or even fountains and waterfalls like those of the Villa d'Este, and if there is not even enough water available to evoke a hazy memory, then we should make use of plants with a weeping habit to give the momentary illusion of fountains: wisteria (left), *Buddleia alternifolia*, or in a park, weeping willow or Deodar cedar (*Cedrus deodara*).

The search for a meaning

"We must compose landscapes to interest the eye and spirit at the same time."
(from "An essay on landscape", R-L. Girardin, 1775)

"A treasure in it is concealed . . ."
(from "The plowman and his sons," *Fables of Jean de la Fontaine*, 1668)

The recurring question "Why is it beautiful?" refers to the inner sensitivity of anyone who is moved to a greater or lesser degree by the sweetness or strength of a composition.

Analysis of vision

Among recent research on optical phenomena, in particular those related to gardens, various types of illusion can be identified that are calculated to make us "see" a space as larger than it appears. (See Richard L. Gregory, *Eye and Brain: The Psychology of Seeing* Princeton University Press, 5th ed., 1997.) In the preceding chapters we have identified a large number of remarkable functions linked, on the one hand, to the physical nature of our environment and, on the other, to physiological signals transmitted by certain parts of the eye. Richard Gregory has identified two other sources of information that contribute to visualization. The first is the accumulation of knowledge acquired from early childhood which we apply to what we see to help us recognize it; of course, this can in some cases make us believe the moon is made of green cheese. The second is what Gregory calls a system of "lateral" rules that the brain uses in a concomitant and incidental manner. This can lead us to "create the world in our image"—for example, by misuse of an excessive concern for geometry.

Illusions are not simply the result of distortions of a physical nature but also, to a large extent, the result of the fact that the brain interprets data that the senses transmit. This is why the meaning we attach, consciously or not, to a particular object (or type of garden) is a highly personal matter.

Good taste, bad taste

Let us therefore put an end to the endless disputes between those who think that "anything goes" (what the French call *bouillon de culture*: a sort of "culture medium" or "broth") and those who are unconditional supporters of a single, unique "good taste."

On one side are those who think that we can ignore human physical and physiological facts and that their only importance is the meaning we give them—never mind the senses; what matters is the sense. A leap, then, toward total liberation, and this without a safety net. On the other side are those who hold the untenable position of believing only in their own "good taste."

Why not consider this apparent opposition in a different way? The formation, or acquisition, of our taste legitimately differentiates us from one civilization to another, from one era to another, from one style of garden to another, and even from one individual to another. But we cannot ignore facts that are inherent in the physiological nature of our species (unless and until it mutates into something else!). Therefore the use of perspective and what are pejoratively called "classical" patterns can be easily detected in many forms of so-called modern or contemporary art.

Meaning and consciousness

The meaning we give to elements of our own decor (photography, sculpture, color choices, clothing) is absolutely personal. The formation of particular analogous groups of neurons takes place throughout our lives and makes us unique as individuals. Therefore, it would be futile to try to establish a set of rigid standards for gardens. As far as this is concerned, ecumenism is the rule. For one person, a simple symbol will be a gateway to a wider emotional or intellectual world, while the same symbol will mean nothing at all to others. Only certain archetypes, associated with dreamlike images, are able to reach the majority of people. But are dream images the same for all civilizations? If we attribute to the horse, for example, the very image of the life force, will this animal have the same meaning for others? Unfortunately, many of the symbolic forms chosen for public gardens mean nothing at all to the great majority of people, with the result that the form's purpose is no more than decorative or insignificant.

Above: A bridge like a delicate transition from one world to another, beyond the passage of time (Ozzie Johnson's garden in Atlanta, Georgia)

Opposite: The quizzical look on the face of a statue makes us feel the same way. (The Greenhouse, Chertsey, England)

Primary functions at work

There is a Jungian theory that even according to Jung himself, is probably less than perfect but that nevertheless has the merit of explaining some of our behavior.

Our functions can be divided into two groups of two: two intellectual functions (thought and sentiment), and two sensory functions (feeling and intuition). In each of these groups one function is dominant, the other secondary. The pairs of dominant and secondary functions are different in different individuals, so mathematically this yields eight different possibilities. Thus people who are dominated by the sensory function will focus on scents, tastes, textures, and colors in their gardens, while others who are intellectual rather than sensory will find meaning in sophisticated compositions and in developed and highly symbolic geometry.

Those driven mainly by sentiment will put into their gardens a thousand memories of loved ones and places visited in the past, conveying emotions they have experienced or moral sentiments they have felt. Finally, others with strong intuition will delight in music, poetry, and bright views and will reserve spaces for spiritual experiences in their gardens. By contrast, secondary functions tend to be asserted in a heavy and unrefined way, awkwardly mimicking what the dominant functions have no difficulty expressing. We should not force our natures into doing things that are not natural for them.

Gardens with meaning

Gardens can take on all kinds of meanings: gardens of the five senses; collectors' gardens; theater gardens; water gardens; exotic gardens; botanical gardens; zoological gardens; floral parks; theme parks. The number of possibilities is infinite, and it is certainly not the purpose of this book to provide an exhaustive list. Therefore, we will content ourselves with addressing only what they sometimes have in common.

To let lions loose, you need to have a setting like this. (Jardin d'Angélique)

Sacred objects

Sacred statues and other objects can only be sacred to the extent that they promote a sense of sacredness in us. This is where we find justification for these particular forms of art, which can be admired in many museums whether they represent Western or Eastern art. The destruction of such works of art is an insult to the whole of humanity.

Curiously, some statues are more impressive than others. Is it because they themselves are unique or because they have acquired a sacred patina, born from the reverence shown to them by generations over time?

The exact positioning of statues in the garden is of the utmost importance. At the intersections of visual lines (some would also say lines of force), there are sites of distinction: focal points that we should know how to identify and make use of, whether for statues or sacred objects such as lanterns, bird baths, ritual instruments, or symbolic stones.

The beauty or precious appearance of an object can cause us to feel respect born of wonder, respect that itself creates a sense of distance.

Apelles Fenosa's violinist plays a tune for us about the beauty of the tall lilies nodding their heads toward her. (Bois des Moutiers)

The emotional dimension: good for the eyes, good for the heart

Some gardens are good for our minds; others are extremely moving.

What touches the heart, by its nature, does so immediately and is part of a world that the intellect will try in vain to explain.

The dimension that gives particular meaning to a garden is that of the affection that its creator devotes to every detail and nuance. Visitors immediately notice the attention to the smallest signs, the general harmony offended by no incongruities or eyesores, the beauty of the ideas, the loving way that trees and shrubs have been pruned to respect the elegance of line, the careful raking of paths, the softness of turf. It is therefore not surprising that the absence of the "eye" of the mistress or master of the garden, even for a few days, is immediately noticeable. How much more so, then, when this eye disappears forever.

The meaning given by a personal relationship with nature

The wonder that comes from contemplating natural beauty can give rise to a taste for horticulture and, through it, the desire to better know the secrets of nature. Learning about gardening teaches us to be humble but also to be curious about what is unknown. Successes, sometimes unexpected, bring forth a cry of recognition in the heart; a privileged path, perhaps, toward the author of all things, the master of harmony.

If nature, revealed to us in this way, made available in its richness and diversity, keeps us from boredom and seems purposely created to solicit our senses and our skills, it is because we cannot live without it. Any disruption of this nature affects us directly:

droughts, floods, excessive temperatures, pollution of all kinds—all are linked to our well-being.

Thus gardens, in addition to being a suitable means of softening manners, are also a school of respect for nature, which is the subject of so many concerns nowadays.

Mankind, trying to describe the sky, is often obliged to speak in terms of "heavenly" music, "divine" singing, or "paradise" gardens. This is just an attempt to express something of the joy felt when approaching communion with what can only be defined as the spiritual realm—a foretaste of much vaster, mysterious joys.

Once we have succeeded in harmonizing our immediate environment, we no longer find ourselves in the situation of being perpetually attacked, always on the defensive. We are then available to lift up our eyes and hearts, ready for unexpected encounters. George Bernard Shaw said, "the best place to find God is in a garden." At least we can offer to our friends and other passing angels a place of rest and rejuvenation, a place for interchange and happiness. Is not this the best meaning we can possibly give to our gardens?

We can see glories in the sky that give us an idea of the grandeur of creation and its author.

Conclusion

"Here we feel plenitude, far from the multitude."
Karlfried Graf von Dürckheim (visiting in the "Valley of the hollow oak" at Bois des Moutiers)

Awakening and bringing energy

Lines, shapes, scale, and colors may all be used to favor depth, transparency, and movement. They have the effect of attracting our eyes and keeping us in a waking state.

In other parts of the world, the awakening of the attention is further stimulated by other means—such as the sharp and regular tapping of one bamboo against another, or the thump of the Japanese Shishi Odoshi water feature (the bamboo that regularly rocks back under the weight of water that fills it), or the sudden squirting of unexpected jets of water, as in gardens of the Italian Renaissance.

The awakening of the senses helps to release a powerful energy.

Harmony-inducing dreams

In a well-ordered garden, harmonious proportions, scents, colors, and sounds pre-dominate. The mind is not distracted by incongruous elements; it is liberated, free to escape in peace toward the heights of consciousness: dreams and poetry. There is nothing surprising about this: every day on the roads we are governed by a coded order learned and recognized by all. Without its existence no one would dare to relax their attention for an instant, let alone begin to dream.

The intellectual barrier

For some historical reason, no doubt a reaction against an abusive spiritual power, many generations have been imbued with a visceral distrust of anything involving communion with nature, instantly dubbed "romanticism." People need to be stuffed with facts to defend themselves against feeling anything. "How many acres is this garden?" "How many gardeners are there?" "How tall is that rhododendron? Is it flowering at the moment?" (sic!)

There is a curious link between this rationalist attitude and that of some non-feeling religions which, for questionable theological reasons, condemn or ridicule, among others, "lovers of little flowers."

"The eye is the lamp of the body; so then if your eye is clear, your whole body will be full of light."

(Matthew 6: 22)

"Beatitude itself is based upon the act of seeing, not on that of love, which follows after."

(Dante, *Paradiso*, canto xxviii, 109)

"The park is like a forgotten place that never stops remembering."
Nadèjda Garrel about Bois des Moutiers (*Le chemin d'Ariane*)

If humanity had to be prevented at all costs from seeing the beauty of creation, it would be hard to do so in a more effective way than this.

Clear or impaired vision

The astonishing verse from the Bible quoted above speaks about the good condition of our eyes as being a prerequisite for the state of "illumination" inside our bodies. This is because our eyes are intermediaries, media that can obscure the quality of our vision both literally and figuratively. Perhaps their ability to see has been affected by a depressive disorder or harmful substances, or else they reveal a kind of malaise (fears, emotional problems, anger making us "see red!").

No matter how beautiful a garden is, it cannot bring sight to the visually impaired, even if the impairment is only mental. In this regard, many of our contemporaries are partly visually impaired. Subjected to aggression from all sides, our eyes have become accustomed to looking aside or have been worn out by contact with increasingly violent images. An intellectual protective barrier has now been established that must be broken down if we are to get back our full visual capacity.

By nature we are ultra-sensitive to our environment, like a priceless Stradivarius mistreated by a mechanical world made of artificial materials and brutal enticements. This leads to a partial anesthesia, a loss of sensitivity, and, ultimately, the beginning of spiritual death. Some try to liberate themselves from this frustration in an outburst of violence, others by undergoing analysis and/or by seeking help of a spiritual nature.

The awakening of the way we see leads us to rediscover ourselves, to regain the use of our senses, to breathe naturally; and this in turn improves the quality of our vision. Our eyes once again become "the lamp of the body."

When we are touched by the harmony or the extreme beauty of a musical creation, a work of art, a garden, or a natural scene, it makes our vision of the world grow and produces a song of happiness in us that we will continually want to share.

Appendices

By Yves Poinsot

Scale, human dimensions, and the old measurements

If we consider gardens as architecture applied to plants, the definition of scale in architecture may also be applied to gardens. The modern Italian architect and teacher Bruno Zevi (1918–2000) defined architectural scale as "the dimensional relationship between a building or part of a building and the human being, who is considered as the measurement of reference." All we have to do is replace "building or part of a building" with "garden or garden feature."

The art of the garden is an ancient one, so why not make use of it to create a new version of the old measurements, tried and tested over many centuries, such as the foot, the span, the cubit, the fathom, and the inch?

If we use these old measurements, provided we make them compatible with the metric system by adapting them to meters and centimeters, it is likely that they will harmonize better with our bodies because most of them are simple fractions of one another. Gardens designed in this way could fit us like tailor-made suits. (See illustrations.)

The new measurement system derived from the old measurements is called the "sapiens system," from *Homo sapiens sapiens*: the species to which we all belong.

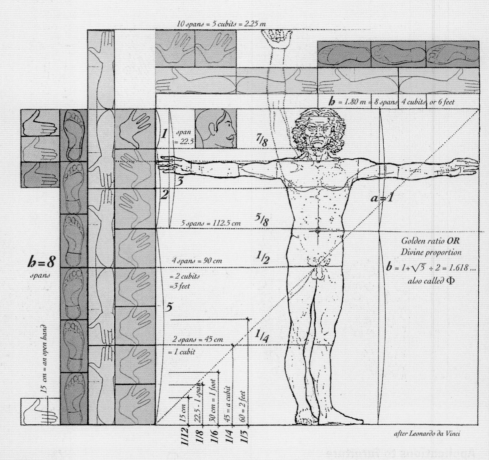

10 *spans* = 5 *cubits* = 2.25 m

b = 1.80 m = 8 *spans* 4 *cubits* or 6 *feet*

1 *span* = 22.5

7/8

3

2

5 *spans* = 112.5 cm

5/8

$b = 8$ *spans*

4 *spans* = 90 cm

1/2

= 2 *cubits* = 3 *feet*

a = 1

Golden ratio **OR** Divine proportion

$b = 1 + \sqrt{5} \div 2 = 1.618\ldots$ also called Φ

5

2 *spans* = 45 cm = 1 *cubit*

1/4

15 cm = an open hand

15 cm = 1 *span*

22.5 = 1 *span*

30 cm = 1 *foot*

45 = a *cubit*

60 = 2 *feet*

1/12 1/8 1/6 1/4 1/3

after Leonardo da Vinci

It is close to the Anglo-Saxon system of feet and inches on a slightly reduced scale, the English foot of 30.5 cm being reduced to 30 cm. This is true for other dimensions: the fathom, 6 feet, shifts from 1.83 m to 1.80 m. The main unit is the sapiens: 1.80 m, the theoretical height of a man, so a half

sapiens is 90 cm; a third, 60; a quarter, 45; a sixth or a foot, 30 cm; an eighth or a span, 22.5; and a twelfth of a foot, or an inch, 2.5 cm. Below this, we return to the millimeter.

This study was also largely inspired by Le Corbusier's "Modulor" anthropometric scale of proportions.

Applications of human dimensions to garden features

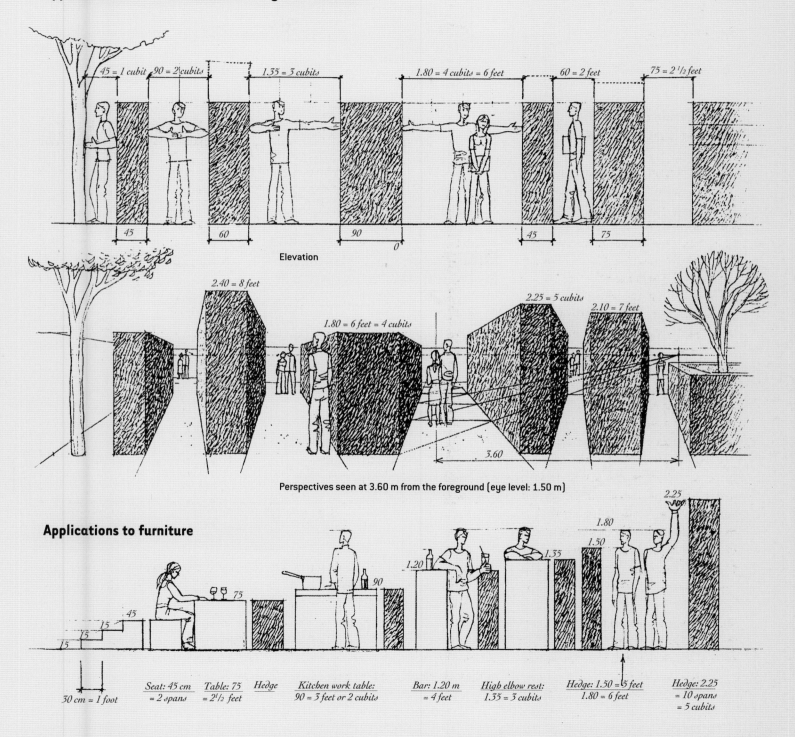

45 = 1 cubit   90 = 2 cubits   1.35 = 3 cubits   1.80 = 4 cubits = 6 feet   60 = 2 feet   75 = 2 ¹/₂ feet

45   60   90   0   45   75

Elevation

2.40 = 8 feet   1.80 = 6 feet = 4 cubits   2.25 = 5 cubits   2.10 = 7 feet

3.60

Perspectives seen at 3.60 m from the foreground (eye level: 1.50 m)

Applications to furniture

2.25

1.80

1.50

1.35

1.20

90

75

45

15

15

15

15

30 cm = 1 foot   Seat: 45 cm = 2 spans   Table: 75 = 2¹/₂ feet   Hedge   Kitchen work table: 90 = 3 feet or 2 cubits   Bar: 1.20 m = 4 feet   High elbow rest: 1.35 = 3 cubits   Hedge: 1.50 = 5 feet 1.80 = 6 feet   Hedge: 2.25 = 10 spans = 5 cubits

Optical illusion: Exaggerated perspective

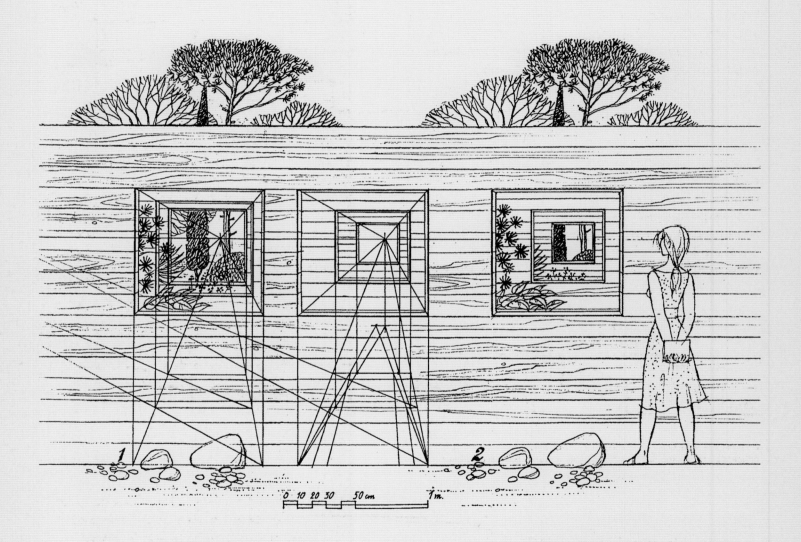

Windows, suggesting a certain depth, are made in three parallel screens. On the right-hand side the windows seem much farther apart than on the left, yet in fact the distance is the same. The illusion comes from the progressive narrowing of the windows on the right, which measure, from front to back, 90, 70 and 50 cm, while those on the left all measure 90 cm.

Stairs: Blondel's formula

This formula is attributed to Francois Blondel, a French architect and theorist (1618–1686), to determine the optimal proportions of the steps of a staircase according to their height. It reads as follows:

2H + T must be between 60 and 65 cm: i.e., $60 \leq 2H + G \leq 65$ cm where H is the riser, or height of the step, and T is the tread, or horizontal depth.

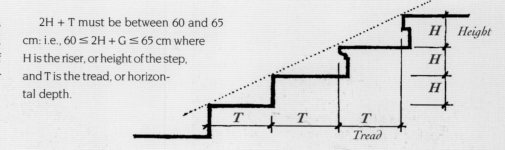

This formula is valid for both indoor and outdoor steps; it is recommended, however, to use gentler slopes outside.

If we follow the formula, the lower the step height, the wider the tread is. In addition, the gentler the slope, the more the sum 2H + T should tend toward the maximum length of

65 cm, or even beyond. Thus if steps of 15 x 30 cm (2H + T = 60) are acceptable, those of 15 x 35 cm are preferable; these are the dimensions of the steps of the wharf leading to the train station on the Grand Canal in Venice. This slope is very agreeable to walk on and would be ideal for a garden.

It is the same for the steps of the Museum of Modern Art in Paris. Conversely, indoors, where there is less space, steeper slopes can be used, with a 2H + T up to 60 cm. The extreme case is that of 20 x 20 stairs, which would be acceptable to access a loft, for example.

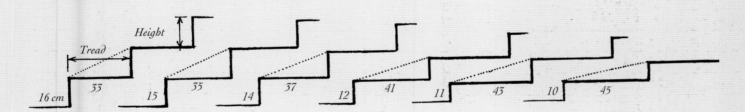

Changing the width of the tread according to the height of the step. In these different examples, the sum 2H + T is constant and always equal to 65 cm.

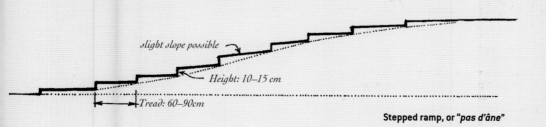

Stepped ramp, or "pas d'âne"

If the ground is naturally sloping—not enough to justify building a traditional staircase, yet too much to be left unchanged—a stepped ramp, or what the French call "donkey steps" (*pas d'âne*), can be installed. In this case, Blondel's formula no longer applies, and tread width can be increased from 60 to 90 cm.

Postscript

A number of events have occurred since this book was reissued in 2008. Recently was the death of Richard L. Gregory, author of *Eye and Brain*, which triggered the urge to write this book about the way we envision gardens. Following this, the success of the Shamrock Garden (the French National Hydrangea Collection) in Varengeville-sur-Mer has put into practice some of the ideas about perspective and colors presented in thisw book.

A new optical effect has been observed in this garden that is related to the apparent abundance of color impressions received by the visitor. This effect manifests itself by a kind of emotional dizziness or the loss of any intellectual reference. In the past it has been named Stendhal Syndrome, because this author was probably the first to describe it. We believe that the effect should at least be mentioned in this new edition.

Other books will doubtless appear on the subject, but we hope that one day a scientist will look into the law that governs the effect of transparency, to assess to what extent transparency is a function of the distance between the observer and the observed object, of the extent to which the object is lit, and of the spacing between the elements that constitute it (the bars of a railing or the mesh of a net, for instance). Once this is understood, it could find application in many ways, in gardens and elsewhere.

It is our hope that now many more creators of gardens, both amateur and professional, will be able to discover the endless possibilities offered by this form of art, the art of gardens.

Manufacturing by KHL Printing
Book design by Mateo Baronnet
Composition: Joe Lops
Production manager: Leeann Graham

ISBN: 978-0-393-73342-6 (pbk.)

W. W. Norton & Company, Inc.,
500 Fifth Avenue, New York, N.Y. 10110
www.wwnorton.com

W. W. Norton & Company Ltd.,
Castle House, 75/76 Wells Street, London W1T 3QT

0 9 8 7 6 5 4 3 2 1

Library of Congress Cataloging-in-Publication Data

Mallet, Robert.

[Optique des jardins. English]

Envisioning the garden : line, scale, distance, form, color, and meaning / Robert Mallet ; drawings by Yves Poinsot ; translation by Bryan Woy.

p. cm.

Originally published in French as: L'Optique des jardins: elargir l'espace, libérer l'esprit.

Includes index.

ISBN 978-0-393-73342-6 (pbk.)

1. Gardens—Design. 2. Landscape architecture. I. Poinsot, Yves. II. Title.

SB473.M27513 2011

712.01—dc22

2010051396

Photo Credits

Robert Mallet : pp. 4, 9, 10, 15l, 15r, 17t, 18t, 18b, 19, 23t, 23b, 24, 26t, 31r, 32t, 32b, 37, 39, 43t, 43b, 44l, 44r, 46l, 51t, 51b, 52b, 55, 58, 62t, 62bl, 62br, 64t, 64b, 65, 66l, 66r, 68b, 70, 71, 72, 73, 74l, 75, 77, 80, 82t, 82b, 83t, 83br, 84t, 84b, 85t, 85b, 86t, 86b, 87, 88l, 88r, 89t, 89b, 90, 91t, 95t, 95b, 97, 99, 100, 101, 102, 103, 105t, 105b, 106, 107, 108t, 108b, 109l, 109r, 110t, 110b, 111, 112, 113, 114, 115, 116, 117, 120, 121, 122tr, 123t, 123b, 125, 127, 128, 129, 131, 132, 133, 134, 135, 136, 137, 139.

Philippe Ferret : pp. 2, 6, 11, 13, 16t, 16b, 17b, 20l, 20r, 22, 26bl, 26br, 27, 31l, 34l, 34r, 40, 41, 45, 46r, 47, 50, 52, 53, 60, 61, 63, 67, 68t, 69, 74r, 78, 79, 81, 83bl, 91b, 92b, 93, 94, 104, 122tl.

Yves Poinsot : pp. 30l, 30r, 33, 36l, 36r, 38l, 38m, 38r, 92t.

Gartenbildagentur Strauß : p.14 (Howard Rice).

Madame figaro/Alexandre Weinberger : pp. 118, 119.